The Crimean Nexus

The Crimean Nexus

Putin's War and the
Clash of Civilizations

CONSTANTINE PLESHAKOV

Yale UNIVERSITY PRESS

New Haven & London

Yale University Press books may be purchased in quantity for educational,
business, or promotional use. For information, please e-mail
sales.press@yale.edu (U.S. office) or sales@yaleup.co.uk (U.K. office).

Set in Janson Roman type by Integrated Publishing Solutions.
Printed in the United States of America.

ISBN 978-0-300-21488-8
Library of Congress Control Number 2016942780

A catalogue record for this book is available from the British Library.

This paper meets the requirements of ANSI/NISO Z39.48-1992
(Permanence of Paper).

10 9 8 7 6 5 4 3 2 1

Mordarka
(blessed are the gentle)

Contents

Contents

The Crimean Nexus

Green Isle, Paradise Lost

Not everyone can find the Crimean peninsula on a map, but once you do, its shape, like that of Italy, is hard to forget. Variously compared to a leaf, a stingray, a pendant, and an eagle, it barely touches on the continent, protruding with almost perfect geometrical precision into the center of the Black Sea.

The thin stem making Crimea *not* an island is called Perekop Isthmus. The Black Sea squeezes it from the west, and Sivash, a bay of the Sea of Azov, from the east. Sivash is not really a bay but rather a shape-shifting conglomerate of lakes, islets, and shoals about forty miles wide whose silt, salt, and mud contours have changed numerous times within human memory.

The road to Kiev runs through Perekop, a bottleneck only four miles wide—roughly the distance between Fourteenth and Ninety-sixth streets in Manhattan. The other dry-land connection to the mainland is a short man-made bridge across the Sivash; that road takes you to Moscow. Close the two connections, and Crimea would effectively become an island.

Entering Crimea is a joy. One moment you are on the plowed-up steppe, enduring five hours of monotony by train or car; then, in a split second, you are on a thin strip of land, barely wide enough to support the road, and there are sea bays all around, as far as the eye can see. The pink, blue, and green coves, flats, shoals, and promontories are all hazy, uncertain, tentative; ebbing and flowing. In a moment you start actually smelling the haze. God help you if your train slows down or your car stalls, because Sivash emits sulfur dioxide. In plain language, it reeks. The Turkic name Sivash means "dirt"; in Slavic languages, the bay is equally uncharitably but realistically known as Gniloye More—the Rotten Sea.

Once past Sivash, you find yourself back on the steppe, not quite distinguishable from the one you left half an hour before; perhaps it looks a shade softer and greener, but that may be only your expectant mood, a result, in the words of an early traveler, of "those paradisiacal ideas" you had formed of the peninsula's beauty. Here the peninsula swells, its two wings unfolding, the western to Cape Tarkhankut, the eastern to Kerch Strait; to the south there are mountains, and beyond them the subtropical South Shore, the area you are very likely headed toward, because that's what most people come to Crimea for: the glittering resort town of Yalta, and the naval legend, the City of the Russian Glory, Sevastopol.[1]

Not terribly tall—a mile at most—the Crimean Mountains are still not to be taken lightly. Erosion of the limestone they are made of has turned the range into a wall. Of the three roads traversing it, two are closed by the snow between November and April. A trekker has more options, but those are not numerous either: the southern side of the range is a cliff; the few canyons are too rocky and slippery for a human to negotiate comfortably; depending on your definition of a mountain pass, there are three to seven notches, which cannot be discovered without extensive homework or a day or two of painful stumbling around.

The ridge is cut into five plateaus still bearing Greek or Turkic names: Ai Petri, Babughan, Chatyr Dagh, Demerdji, Karabi. These plateaus are separated by gorges, and to get from plateau A to plateau B you have to follow the gorge edge, a detour easily taking half a day. On the plateaus, rain and wind have eaten up most of the soil, leaving a barren surface studded with vertically standing limestone arrows, or "dragon teeth" in local speak. There is no water to be found on the plateaus in summertime, except in caves.

Across the ridge sits the subtropical littoral, commonly referred to as the South Shore: orchards, castles, palaces, whitewashed villages, parks; beaches, fruit markets, sweet wine; sunburn, queues, peddlers, souvenirs, nightlife.

Crimea is fully maritime, and it is possible to chart its past through the stories of the shipwrecks sitting on the seabed around its coasts: Athenian, Roman, Byzantine, Genoese; British in the Crimean War, Soviet in World War II. The sea has had many names, always with some unwelcoming connotation. The name the Greeks gave it, Pontus Axeinos, "Dark," lives today as Kara Deniz in Turkish, Black Sea in English, Chornoye More in Russian, Chorne in Ukrainian, and Marea Neagra in Romanian.[2]

The Black Sea bottom is largely hydrogen sulfide, like oceans of a planet from a science-fiction story. The "largest mass of lifeless water in the world," the author of a Black Sea travelogue, Neal Ascherson, called it. Very low in oxygen, the bottom waters support little life, and that makes it an ideal excavation site for marine archeology: organic matter, such as a ship's hull, decomposes there very slowly, so that artifacts may sit unspoiled for centuries. An unknown scroll covered with Aristotle's handwriting could still be lying in some shipwreck's hold, curling in a sealed amphora, the universal container of antiquity. Deep-sea archeology is extremely costly, and so far just one ancient wreck has been recovered, a Byzantine ship off Turkish Sinop. Christened Sinop

D, it is supposed to be the best-preserved underwater artifact ever found.[3]

The existence of the hydrogen sulfide layer explains the columns of fire reportedly seen rising from the sea after earthquakes. In 2007, an article in a European scientific journal caused a media splash by arguing that the Black Sea was so combustible that if an asteroid ever hit it, the release of fire and gas would annihilate all life along its coasts.[4]

The other sea, the one washing Crimea's eastern shore, Azov, has mud volcanoes. There, the Byzantine Greeks collected *naphtha*, a combustible liquid similar to gasoline, to use in hand grenades, remembered famously as "Greek fire." A nineteenth-century traveler compared the naphtha springs to "the chimneys of the infernal regions, as the crust of the soil is pierced with black holes surmounted by little cones, from whence the mud and gas bubble up together. The whole soil around trembles when walked upon, and one fears to sink into the bowels of the earth." Perhaps because of the naphtha and the volcanoes, one interpretation of Greek myths puts the entrance to Hades on the Azov Sea. Henry James used the sea as a symbol of absolute evil in *The Turn of the Screw*.[5]

Descriptions of Crimea can be found in the texts forming the early Western canon: Homer, Herodotus, Xenophon, Strabo, Pliny. Compared with parts of the eastern Mediterranean such as Peloponnesus or Cyprus, Crimea is not particularly striking, but it is the only chunk of land anywhere near the Mediterranean that Russia and Ukraine have ever owned. Crimea is their only connection to the cradle of the Western world, and this is part of the reason why both nations cling to the peninsula so fiercely.

A random dig in the Crimean soil may turn up chunks of Venetian pottery, an Ottoman coin, and German shrapnel. Every old building in use today was very likely something else in the past: a church was a mosque, a grain depot was a church, a rental slum was a villa, a town library was a customs house. There is hardly a square mile where you would not come across the ruins of past habitats—farms, monasteries, mosques, forts, castles, walled gardens, shepherds' shelters, terraces, wells. It doesn't matter where you go—could be a notch saddling a mountain range or a ravine in the prairie—ruins will be there, signifying that people once lived on that spot before someone came and drove them away or killed them.

To paraphrase Winston Churchill's quip about the Balkans, Crimea has produced more history than it can consume, and as in the Balkans, the excess has led to strife. The perpetual struggle for Crimea has given the peninsula a mythical clout as a "paradise lost" for a surprising range of cultures. The Nazis, for example, believed it was the homeland of Tyrol Germans. With the German boots on the ground in 1941, Hitler renamed Crimea Gotenland and—prematurely as it happened—ordered a repatriation program.

Two devastating wars of the twentieth century—the Russian civil war of 1917–1920 and World War II—brought massacres, deportation, and emigration so massive that today just 10 percent of Crimean families can claim uninterrupted presence on the peninsula going back farther than three generations. Out of today's population of two million, 58 percent identify as Russian, 24 percent as Ukrainian, and 12 percent as Tatar, the remaining 6 percent split among Jews, Greeks, Germans, Armenians, Bulgarians, and Byelorussians.[6]

But what makes the peninsula so appealing for that part of the world that Moscow was willing to sacrifice its place at the table of "civilized" nations to annex it in 2014?

What *is* Crimea?

Climatically, the peninsula is a shard of the Mediterranean, the northernmost subtropics, a Côte d'Azur on the edge of snow and ice. Tatars called it Green Isle; Catherine the Great called it Eden;

an early American visitor said it was "an emerald in a sea of sapphire."[7]

Geopolitically, Crimea is the gateway to the Eurasian heartland. A maritime citadel in the middle of the Black Sea, colonized by every major Mediterranean power from the Romans to the Ottomans, Crimea allows an empire to project its presence onto the Caucasus and the Middle East. Whoever rules Crimea commands the Black Sea, and who rules the Black Sea commands the continental trade routes between the Balkans and China. The famed Silk Road started in the Crimean port of Kaffa (today's Feodosia). In the twenty-first century, the Black Sea is an energy connector. Fifty tankers a day sail through the Bosporus, and the Blue Stream pipeline brings Russian natural gas to Turkey. Currently, Moscow is pushing for a megaproject, a trans–Black Sea pipeline that would deliver Russian gas straight to southern Europe.

Culturally, Crimea sits on a great divide between "East" and "West," where European Christendom meets the Middle Eastern lands of Islam. In the twenty-first century, it is where NATO and the European Union's territory comes in contact with Eurasian heartlands. The ongoing conflict in Ukraine involves Russia and the West; in Crimea, it is tripartite because Crimea is as much a part of the Islamic world as it is part of the West and Russia. Unsurprisingly, Crimea's identity is transient, fleeting, ever evolving, never reaching a final point. Each culture sees its own Crimea.

All of this makes Crimea a linchpin of Eurasian security, a flashpoint of conflicting ideologies, and a petri dish for figuring out the rules of engagement in the new cold war.

The conflict has been in the making for a very long time. Neal Ascherson wrote in 1996 that the Black Sea coasts belonged "to all their people, but also to none of them"; when "some fantasy of national unity" arrives, the "apparent solidarity of centuries can dissolve within days or hours." A territory traditionally prized and contested, a place with no permanent ethnic core, a national fetish for Russians, Ukrainians, and Tatars, Crimea has long been a time bomb. When the bomb went off in 2014, it jump-started the separatists' insurgency in eastern Ukraine and sent waves of foreboding throughout Eastern Europe.[8]

In his World War II memoir *Lost Victories*, the German field marshal Erich von Manstein recalls the funeral of his "truest comrade of all," the driver Fritz Nagel, a man with "frank brown eyes" who was killed in an air raid in the summer of 1942. "We buried him," Manstein writes, "alongside all our other German and Italian comrades in the Yalta cemetery high above the sea—perhaps one of the most lovely spots on the whole of that glorious coastline."[9] Five years later, my grandfather died in Yalta, and in all honesty, I cannot be sure that the 1947 graves were not dug on top of the graves of the Axis soldiers. Three years after the occupation, enemy burials were not something people in Eastern Europe respected or honored.

My mother was ten at the time, my grandmother thirty-three, the dead man thirty-two.

I am a third-generation Crimean, a fact that makes me suspect in the eyes of every warring faction. I am expected to know where my allegiances are, and I don't. According to my U.S. passport, I was born in Ukraine; my certificate of naturalization lists my previous citizenship as "Russian"; some older immigration documents suggest I come from the USSR.

Like so many others, ours was a family of mutts. It depresses me to hear how casually many people from that part of the world call themselves "Russian" or "Ukrainian." *Ethnicity* is an empty word, and *culture* is hardly better. In the end it is little more than the mother tongue and an idiosyncratic set of prejudices.

Because the archives in the former USSR are only partially open to the public, it is a miracle I was able to trace our family roots to the late eighteenth century. According to the information I now have, my ancestors practiced Eastern Orthodox Christianity, Islam, Old Rite Eastern Christianity, and shamanism; the languages they spoke included Mari (a Finno-Ugric cousin of Hungarian and Finnish), Romanian, Russian, and Ukrainian. A Ukrainian archpriest, a Romanian schoolteacher, a Russian shopkeeper, a Cossack farmer—all, presumably, hyperconscious of their ethnicity and class, they could not possibly have imagined that their children would intermarry. Made only briefly possible by Marxist cosmopolitanism, the theory and practice of the melting pot did not last, and two generations later the former Soviets are at least as concerned about their bloodlines as their forebears were a century earlier.

Inauspiciously, our family geography coincides with the 2014–2016 war zone—Crimea and eastern Ukraine, or Donbass. My grandparents met on the coal mines of Luhansk; the year was 1934 and both were engineers, grandma among the first in that traditionally male profession. My mother was born in a company town with the futuristic name of Krasnyi Luch, or Red Ray. Then there was a transfer to a power plant in Sevastopol, then war, German air raids, occupation, famine, deaths in the family. In the summer of 1942, grandma had to walk from Yalta to Sevastopol: she hoped she would be able to find her sister, a Red Army nurse who might have survived the siege of Sevastopol and could be hiding in the ruins of the city. Dead tired after walking the first twenty miles, she did a thing a young woman should not have done in an occupied country under any circumstances: she tried hitchhiking. The German driver who stopped was in a sarcastic mood. "Give you a ride? Give *you* a ride?" he said. "See that?" and he pointed at the German soldiers' graves stretching along the curb as far as the eye could see. "When my brothers rise, *then* I will give you a ride. Now go fetch one from Stalin."

As I am writing this, the town of Krasnyi Luch is again in a war zone. Sevastopol seems to have been reduced to a symbol; Russian imperial glory or Ukrainian sovereignty, its meaning is not its people but a bigger concept, at the moment strangely accepted as something worthier. The Crimean power grid, Krymenergo, which my grandparents helped to build, now operates virtually on an island, cut off from the mainland by the 2014 annexation, and as a result suffers one blackout after another. Disconnect, alienation, absurdity.

Our house in Yalta was just five minutes' walk from a villa once occupied by Anton Chekhov (who, it must be said, detested Yalta, a sleepy strange place that was supposed to ease his tuberculosis but didn't). Since his day, the neighborhood had changed. The river running through our little valley never flooded anymore, even when the snows melted, because most of its water was now siphoned off for irrigation. On the other side of the river, where in Chekhov's day a Romanov grand duchess lived, now our power plant stood. The river had been given a new Russian name, but everyone still called it the Uchan Su, Turkic for "streaming water."

In Chekhov's time, Autka, as our neighborhood was called, had been largely Tatar and Greek, but in 1944 Stalin ordered the minorities deported, and the only reason our family did not live in somebody else's home was that our apartment building was recent. In Crimea, we resembled what the French people call *pieds-noirs*, referring to the generations of Europeans living in colonized North Africa and calling it home.

I first met an American forty years ago on the Yalta promenade. She was a passenger from a cruise ship that had docked in our little port that morning; I was fourteen or fifteen at the time. The conversation had little substance, yet the encounter made me the first person in our family ever to speak to an American. We read that as a sign of hope: a better world seemed to be hatching. Western cruise ships were becoming a familiar sight, Americans were allowed to explore the town unchaperoned, and in Yalta's western cove, Soviet leaders entertained Richard Nixon.

Things were going so well that, forty years later, we thought, Americans would be buying properties along Crimea's coast and travel agencies would sell packages to the "Black Sea Riviera." A better world could have hatched, but it did not. Instead, America and Russia have sleepwalked into another cold war.

The clash is again ideological, only instead of Communism, Russia now promotes a pure and holy "special Russian way." As before, Moscow is building an international coalition of anti-American underdogs. The fight for spheres of influence is back, along with another staple Cold War feature—proxy wars. For all intents and purposes, in 2014–2016 in Ukraine, the insurgents fought for Putin, and the Kiev government forces for NATO.

It is as if we have been struck by the Tower of Babel curse again. The story told in Genesis starts with the whole world speaking a single language and dreaming of greatness. "Come," people said, "let's make great piles of burnt brick and collect natural asphalt to use as mortar. Let's build a great city with a tower that reaches to the skies—a monument to our greatness! This will bring us together and keep us from scattering all over the world." As we know, the project was not finished: alarmed by the new power of humans, God gave them "different languages," and that proved enough to rekindle discord.[10]

The early 1990s were the time when the world probably came closest to speaking a single language. The collapse of communism in the Soviet Union, according to the political theorist Samuel Huntington, had generated the "belief that a global democratic revolution was underway and that in short order Western concepts of human rights and Western forms of political democracy would prevail throughout the world." Francis Fukuyama announced that history, as a contest of ideas, had ended and that liberal democracy had proved itself the fittest. Yet since then, we have somehow lost the shared language, and now the same word—"democracy," "progress," or "nationalism"—carries different meanings depending on who utters it.[11]

Today, writes Robert Kagan in the *New Republic*, "the signs of the global order breaking down are all around us." Twenty-five years after we buried the Cold War, the BBC news site finds it acceptable to publish a plane spotter's article called "How to tell if a Russian bomber is flying overhead."[12]

In a book published in 1995, the then U.S. ambassador to Ukraine, William Miller, wrote: "Inclusion, consensus, and the absence of violence have been hallmarks of Ukrainian politics, producing an atmosphere of political stability in which extremism has been all but avoided."[13] On a chance visit to the American embassy in Kiev a year later, that was what I heard from Ambassador Miller and other diplomats. At the time, it was hard to disagree with that optimistic assessment. Two decades later, it sounds like the description of a different country.

On the same trip in 1996 I revisited Crimea. The people I met were preoccupied with two ills: sudden impoverishment and organized crime. People I had grown up with were now selling rubbish in a flea market. The Ukrainian currency was so weak that cashiers, forced to accept wads of cash, did not even bother to count the bills, let alone check them for (numerous) forgeries; they just dumped them into the register with the look of tired resignation.

Mobsters from every corner of the diseased state had descended upon Crimea's South Shore like hungry scavengers. In Yalta, we were the only customers in our hotel because the manager had been gunned down in the lobby two days before. The only antique dealership in town had been bombed into dust. Better restaurants were closed for "private parties," and in all the lesser food joints stray dogs, begging for food, kept you company. The favorite café of my childhood, Little Bee, was now a casino called Third Rome. All but three of the former Romanov palaces on the coast had been appropriated by the mob. One had a sign on the gate: "Don't stop. Guards open fire without warning." Mobsters had designated one particular stretch of the coastal highway as a meeting place, and when their BMWs stopped there right in the middle of the road for chitchat, traffic in both directions froze—no honking, no arguing, not a peep, not even from the habitually short-fused truck drivers.

That free-for-all had a strange feeling of timelessness to it. A lost island, a pirates' republic, a territory off the maps, forgetting the world, and seemingly already forgotten by it.

In restaurants, scantily dressed women sold rare Alpine flowers. Fresh fish was back on the menu because industry along the coast remained shut down, and the species had recuperated. Old panting steamboats ferried peddlers to Istanbul and back; the family now occupying our old apartment had turned it into a warehouse for contraband goods. The only person to bring up reunification with Russia was the cemetery worker I had hired to fix my grandfather's tomb. For gravediggers, being a maverick comes with the territory, and I paid little attention to the old man's rumblings.

What I saw made me very angry, because that had been my home. Yet Russia at the time was not faring much better, and as all the ex-Soviets had learned the hard way, transition to a market economy is painful and ugly. Its pains, I thought, were not something Crimea, the rest of Ukraine, or Russia would be unable to outgrow. I don't think anyone believed war would come next.

PART I

Terrain

ONE

Tower of Babel

There seems to be a growing international consensus regarding the origins of the crisis in the east: the involved parties sleepwalked into it, having misinterpreted each other's agendas. Miscommunication that persistent must have had a method to it. To deconstruct it, we shall look at both the approximations—half-truths and honest mistakes—and controversies surrounding basic concepts of international relations, such as spheres of influence.[1]

Approximations

Possibly the biggest approximation fueling the conflict in the east has been a dichotomous approach to almost every aspect: historical, political, cultural, personal. The "us versus them" outlook that prevails in Ukraine, Russia, and the United States turns amorphousness into concrete, gray areas into black-and-white, a quilt into brick.

Too often the current clash between Moscow and Kiev gets presented as a battle between good and evil, with all the complexities, inconsistencies, and absurdities reduced to a Harry Potter level of analysis: Russian president Vladimir Putin is Lord Voldemort, the United States is Dumbledore, and Ukraine takes the role of Harry Potter, the boy who lived. One could only wish the protagonists and their agendas were that well defined.

To begin with, not two but three worlds meet (or, if you prefer, clash) in Ukraine: European, Russian, and Turkic. Like every other stretch of the Black Sea coast, southern Ukraine used to be part of the Ottoman Empire (it was not for nothing that the Black Sea was known as the Ottoman Lake). Yet in each narrative—Ukrainian, Russian, and American—it is "Russia against the West," the adversaries solid, fully formed, definite in their values and intentions. In this discourse, the only sort of agency Ukraine has is the capacity to choose between the two, to eventually join the "right" side. This strange duality misjudges the nature of the protagonists in the conflict and misplaces its context.

Depending on where Ukrainian politicians currently stand on NATO and the European Union, U.S. media tend to describe them as either "pro-Western" good people or "pro-Russian" bad types. The classification is unfortunate, as it originates in the false premise that the main ambition of Ukrainian leaders is to choose between Russia and the West. Of course, this has never been the case. In Ukraine, as anywhere else, politicians exhibit cold pragmatism, healthy manipulative skills, and a praiseworthy inclination to exploit the animosity between great powers to its fullest.

In the vernacular of U.S. media or, for that matter, academia, "pro-Western," or "Westernized" is a compliment, synonymous with "reform" and "progress," even when the signs of Westernization cited and praised are oddly superficial: beer parties in post-Saddam Baghdad, miniskirts in post-Taliban Kabul, McDonald's in post-Soviet Moscow.

Strictly speaking, the term "pro-Western" should not really be part of the foreign policy lexicon: when calling someone "pro-Western," do we mean that he or she is pro-U.S., pro-France, or pro-Germany? Pro-E.U. or pro-NATO? Also, aren't "Western values" time- and place-specific? Is support of, say, gay rights now a mandatory part of being pro-Western? Questions of this sort never end.

With remarkable ease, we classify political movements and public figures in the developing world as either anti- or pro-Western, mistaking intention for commitment and promises for achievements. Not surprisingly, each time a "pro-Western reformer" switches ideological gears or proves corrupt, it leads to handwringing, disillusionment, and a rushed search for a new favorite.

This vicious cycle brings to mind a warning given to the Solidarity movement of the 1980s by the old wise man of Polish politics, Cardinal Stefan Wyszyński: "It's not a question of wanting to change the leaders, it's they who must change. We must make sure—and I make this comparison quite deliberately—that one gang of robbers doesn't steal the keys of the state treasury from another similar gang."[2]

The second approximation dimming our understanding of the crisis is related to nation-building. Every modern state in Eastern Europe is young; all got carved from the territory of a fading empire—Austria-Hungary, Germany, Turkey, Russia. Many descend from greater and mightier entities. Sixteenth-century Poland, for example, was the equal of France, and in the 1610s Polish troops occupied Moscow. Riches-to-rags journeys like that make territorial disputes endemic to the region.

"Self-determination," introduced to Europe by President Woodrow Wilson, was neither comprehensible nor practical. Wilson's own secretary of state, Robert Lansing, posed questions not fully answered a century later: "When the President talks of 'self-determination' what unit has he in mind? Does he mean a race, a territorial area, or a community?" Defining units worthy of self-determination was just one problem among many. As the decision lay with foreign sponsors naturally swayed by self-interest and prejudice, verdicts were arbitrary. Wilson was a champion of independent Poland, but he wanted Ukraine to stay within an undivided, albeit already Communist, Russia. Lansing found the policy geopolitically sound, yet warned that cases like that turned self-determination into a mere phrase: "It will raise hopes which can never be realized. It will, I fear, cost thousands of lives." In cases of "submerged" nations recognized by foreign sponsors, there was no way of establishing their borders in a manner that would be universally found fair because of the past migrations, cleansings, and repatriations. An American participant in the Paris Peace Conference of 1919 that granted nationhood to several Eastern European nations, including two abortive projects—Yugoslavia and Czechoslovakia—wrote: "The 'submerged nations' are coming to the surface and as soon as they appear, they fly at somebody's throat."[3]

Conflicts among formerly "submerged nations" have been going on for more than a century, and the Balkan Wars set the scene for World War I. After World War II, stiffened by the military blocs of the Cold War era, they temporarily reduced in intensity, yet it is still inaccurate to insist, as Robert Kagan does, that "Russia's invasion of Ukraine and seizure of Crimea was the first time since World War II that a nation in Europe had engaged in territorial conquest." In 1974, Turkey and Greece went to war over Cyprus, and the island has been divided into "pro-Turkish" and "pro-Greek" parts ever since.[4]

Many experts, underestimating the difficulties of nation-building in Eastern Europe in the post-Soviet euphoria, also failed to see that Russia was wrestling with nation-building just as painfully as, say, Serbia.

The third problematic approximation concerns the character of modern Ukraine. Difficult for Russians, nation-building is precarious for Ukrainians. Contrary to the well-meaning patriotic mythology, Ukraine was never independent prior to 1991. Its territory is a quilt of lands ceded by (in chronological order) Turkey, Poland, Austria-Hungary, and Russia. It has been a battlefield for the past six centuries. In 1709, Russian tsar Peter the Great and Swedish king Charles XII fought the decisive battle of the Russo-Swedish War in the core of Ukraine, Poltava. After losing the battle, Charles fled to the Ottoman domains close to modern Odessa. It is hard to believe that Sweden's and Turkey's spheres of influence ever overlapped—yet in Ukraine they did. The last time Poles occupied Ukraine's capital city of Kiev was in 1920. What is happening in Ukraine now is tragic, but neither novel nor unexpected, and the more propagandists insist on the intrinsic unity of a Ukrainian nation, the dimmer the prospects for a true settlement.

Transition to sovereignty can be (relatively) smooth only when the birth of a nation-state is preceded by the emergence of a nation. That was certainly not the case with Ukraine. A state but not yet a nation, Ukraine struggles like a forced bulb. In this condition, encouraging it to choose between Russia and Europe means exerting too much pressure on the fragile domestic balance. In 2013–2016, that pressure brought unendurable distress.

Ukraine *is* a divided nation, but its divisions are more intricate than the "pro-European" west and the "pro-Russian" east. Every conflict on its territory involves numerous regional agents. Conflated and fluid local identities make Ukraine's territorial integrity frail. In foreign policy, this makes it a swing state. Domestically, the power of regional actors undercuts the authority of the central government in Kiev. Henry Kissinger writes: "Ukraine has been independent for only 23 years; it had previously been under some kind of foreign rule since the 14th century. Not surprisingly, its leaders have not learned the art of compromise, even less of historical perspective. The politics of post-independence Ukraine clearly demonstrates that the root of the problem lies in efforts by Ukrainian politicians to impose their will on recalcitrant parts of the country, first by one faction, then by the other."[5]

Parties to a long conflict may think of themselves as oil and water that do not mix, but on a territory that keeps changing hands, they do. Ceded for a decade or a century, a region becomes culturally transformed, and when it returns to the country that had lost it, it does so with a new face and character. Several cultures had overlapped on the territory of modern Ukraine, resulting in peculiar, region-specific cultural molds.

It is this state without a nation, unused to independence and self-governance, that has now become subject to the "Monroe doctrines" of regional powers, NATO and European Union eastward expansion, and attempts at regime change.

Monroe Doctrines

Russia responded to the collapse of the USSR with an incarnation of the Monroe Doctrine: all of the former Soviet republics were defined as the "near abroad," and part of Russia's exclusive sphere of influence. All had once shared a continuous human and economic space, and Russia, as the former imperial core, had a particularly big stake in keeping the legacy. Every attempt by a foreign power, whether the United States, China, Iran, Germany, or Turkey, to step into Russia's backyard was deemed poaching, a provocation, brinkmanship. When in 1995 NATO announced plans to expand eastward, Russians reacted as Americans did when Khrushchev put missiles in Cuba.[6]

The "near abroad" concept has been deservedly criticized as neo-imperialist, yet immorality does not necessarily invalidate realpolitik. Many failing empires of the past had cushioned their disintegration precisely by creating a "near abroad." The British

Commonwealth is a good example. Second, contemporary great powers, such as the United States and China, maintain and guard their periphery zealously and determinedly (the United States in the Caribbean, China in Southeast Asia), so it makes little sense to hold Moscow to a higher standard. Finally, in the end of the Cold War, both American and Western European leaders had led Russians to believe that they would have preferred the Soviet Union to stay undivided (minus the Baltic countries, whose right to secede no one in the West doubted). Pretty much like the Entente in 1919, they now suspected that the disintegration would lead to geopolitical chaos. As a veteran of the U.S. Foreign Service, former ambassador Jack F. Matlock, puts it, "The Soviet Union collapsed as a state *despite* the end of the Cold War, not because of it." In 1991, in a speech in Kiev, President George H. W. Bush advised the non-Russian Soviet republics to keep a democratic federation with Moscow. Aggressive U.S. involvement in nation-building in the post-Soviet space would not start until Bill Clinton's presidency.[7]

Just like the Monroe Doctrine, the "near abroad" was a response to new ideological and geopolitical challenges. For the United States in 1823, those challenges came from the reactionary politics of European powers after the downfall of Napoleon, and the formation of the Holy Alliance. For Russia in the 1990s, the ideological challenge was the worldwide triumph of Western universalism, with NATO a new Holy Alliance.[8]

What worried the United States in the 1820s was the possible return of old foes to the Americas, and this is why President James Monroe proclaimed that the American continents were not "to be considered as subjects for future colonization by any European powers." He warned that the United States "should consider any attempt on their part to extend their system to any portion of this hemisphere as dangerous to our peace and security." A similar rationale stood behind the "near abroad": after seventy years of forced absence, Western powers were returning to Eurasian heart-lands.[9]

No newly independent nation in the near abroad is more intertwined with Russia than Ukraine. A Russian ambassador to the United States said that Russia's relations with Ukraine were "identical to those between New York and New Jersey." A deputy foreign minister warned: "Remember, anything between us and the Ukrainians is a family affair, and any disagreement we have is a family feud." The most prominent American realist, Henry Kissinger, concurs: "The West must understand that, to Russia, Ukraine can never be just a foreign country. . . . Even such famed dissidents as Aleksandr Solzhenitsyn and Joseph Brodsky insisted that Ukraine was an integral part of Russian history and, indeed, of Russia."[10]

Russia does not have a right or a duty to remain Ukraine's custodian, and its military and economic superiority are not going to last forever. Nor should Russia's pretentions go unquestioned or unchallenged. The point is that for Russians, Ukraine is part of their continuous national space, not unlike what Canada is for the United States, but even closer.

Eastward Expansion: NATO and the European Union

If we looked for a single factor that pushed Moscow into annexing Crimea and then invading Donbass, NATO's eastward expansion, especially into the former Soviet republics in the Baltics in 2004, would be it.[11]

When NATO was born in 1949, its mission (as famously put by its first secretary-general, Lord Ismay) was "to keep the Russians out, the Americans in, and the Germans down." While keeping the Russians "out" was not necessarily a bad idea, the question remains whether the eastward expansion of the alliance has served the purpose or, alternatively, made things worse.

When the Berlin Wall fell in 1989, the global system of alliances froze in suspense. Even the unification of Germany did not look guaranteed. The prime minister of Italy, Giulio Andreotti, quipped: "We love the Germans so much that the more Germanies there are the better." U.S. secretary of state James A. Baker asked, "Would the Soviets permit a unified German state to remain in NATO, the military alliance that protected the West against Soviet aggression?" Not only the Soviet Union but also France and Britain were doubtful "about the implications for Europe and the world of reconstituting the state responsible for two of the bloodiest wars of the century."[12]

Yet East and West Germany were allowed to merge, with the reunified Germany a NATO country. That was the first expansion of NATO in the post–Cold War world. The administration of George H. W. Bush allegedly assured Mikhail Gorbachev that NATO would stop on the reunified Germany's eastern border. According to several accounts in February 1990, Baker told Gorbachev: "If we maintain a presence in Germany that is a part of NATO, there would be no extension of NATO's jurisdiction for forces of NATO one inch to the east." Later, Baker insisted that he had been misunderstood and that NATO expansion east of Germany simply did not come up in the negotiations. The former U.S. ambassador to the USSR Jack F. Matlock, though not a big fan of NATO enlargement, emphasizes that all there had been was "a general understanding" Bush and Gorbachev reached that "the USSR would not use force in Eastern Europe and the U.S. would not 'take advantage' of changes there. This was not a treaty binding on future governments." This is not to say that the "understanding" was not sincere; it was—but only as long as the two leaders stayed in power. "I am sure," Matlock continues, "that if Bush had been reelected and Gorbachev had remained as president of the USSR there would have been no NATO expansion during their terms in office."[13]

Russian diplomats later accused the United States of breaking a promise, but the fact remains that no one ever unequivocally promised Moscow that NATO would not start taking new members.

The newly independent Eastern European countries demanded NATO membership loudly and emotionally, openly referring to Russia as a threat. In April 1993, the presidents of Poland, the Czech Republic, and Hungary approached President Clinton in person to ask for admission. Their strongest advocate in NATO was German chancellor Helmut Kohl, who argued that NATO could not tell Eastern Europeans they were not welcome "after what they did to survive communism." But in a private conversation with President Clinton's adviser Strobe Talbott in January 1997, Kohl admitted that for Germany NATO expansion was "not just a moral issue," and that it was in Germany's "self-interest to have this development now and not in the future." According to Talbott, Kohl's reasoning amounted to blackmail: as long as Germany sat on the frontier between East and West, he allegedly said, it would be tempted to relapse into extreme nationalism, but if the European Union expanded eastward, making Germany the middle of Europe, not its fringe, all German insecurities would be gone. But the E.U., Kohl stressed, could not expand unless NATO led the way.[14]

If Talbott's rendering is correct, then in buying this logic, the Clinton administration agreed to subsidize European economic dreams with U.S. military clout and American taxpayers' money.

Among the few staunch enthusiasts of NATO enlargement was Bill Clinton's secretary of state, Madeleine Albright. To promote the unpopular cause, in February 1997 she published an essay in *The Economist* called "Enlarging NATO: Why Bigger Is Better." "Those who ask 'where is the threat?' mistake NATO's real value," Albright wrote. "The alliance is not a wild-west posse that we trot out only when danger appears. It is a permanent presence, designed to promote common endeavors and to prevent a threat from ever arising." She claimed that NATO enlargement was not taking place because of a new Russian threat, yet at the same time insisted that Russia could not be allowed to "look at countries like Poland or Estonia or Ukraine as a buffer zone that separates Russia from Europe."

Albright assured readers that "poll after poll has shown that few ordinary Russians express concern about an alliance that many of their leaders concede poses no actual military threat to Russia." Her claim was unsubstantiated, if not outright false. "It would not be in our interest," Albright argued, "to delay or derail enlargement in response to the claims of some Russians that this constitutes an offensive act. Doing so would only encourage the worst political tendencies in Moscow. It would send a message that confrontation with the West pays off." The latter was a mistake in judgment: it was not appeasement, but NATO enlargement, that eventually brought about the "worst political tendencies in Moscow."[15]

The president of Russia, Boris Yeltsin, seemed to regard Clinton's public endorsement of NATO expansion as a personal betrayal. Repeating what Russian analysts across the whole political spectrum had been saying, Yeltsin warned that "the security of all European countries depends on Russia feeling secure." It was not necessary to add that the incorporation of Eastern Europe into NATO did not help Russia feel secure.[16]

Initially, NATO expansion was a hard sell. French president Jacques Chirac complained that it did not take into account "Russian sensitivities." In Washington, outside Clinton's White House almost no one liked it. The Pentagon and the Joint Chiefs of Staff were apoplectic. General Barry McCaffrey warned that if the United States was not careful, Americans would "get ourselves sucked into some godforsaken Eurasian quagmire" that could result in a "shooting war with Russia."[17]

George F. Kennan, the ninety-three-year-old patriarch of U.S.

foreign policy, came out of retirement to denounce the plan as "the most fateful error of American policy in the entire post-cold-war era," in an op-ed piece in the *New York Times*. He predicted that NATO enlargement could be expected to "inflame the nationalistic, anti-Western and militaristic tendencies in Russian opinion; to have an adverse effect on the development of Russian democracy; to restore the atmosphere of the cold war to East-West relations, and to impel Russian foreign policy in directions decidedly not to our liking."[18] In May 1998, after the Senate vote affirming Clinton's NATO plan, Kennan saw the "beginning of a new cold war." "I think the Russians will gradually react quite adversely," he told Thomas L. Friedman of the *New York Times*, "and it will affect their policies. I think it is a tragic mistake. There was no reason for this whatsoever. No one was threatening anybody else. This expansion would make the Founding Fathers of this country turn over in their graves. We have signed up to protect a whole series of countries, even though we have neither the resources nor the intention to do so in any serious way. . . . Don't people understand? Our differences in the cold war were with the Soviet Communist regime. And now we are turning our backs on the very people who mounted the greatest bloodless revolution in history to remove that Soviet regime."[19]

To another influential thinker, Samuel P. Huntington, creating a "new dividing line through Europe" looked logical, justified, and historically inevitable. The "logic of civilizations," he argued, dictated that Poland, the Czech Republic, Slovakia, Hungary, the Baltic republics, Slovenia, and Croatia should join the European Union and NATO. The region thus defined by these organizations "would be coextensive with Western civilization as it has historically existed in Europe." But he opposed extending the alliances to the territories "where Western Christianity ends and Islam and Orthodoxy begin"—including Bulgaria, Romania, Albania, and, of course, Ukraine.[20]

Poland, Hungary, and the Czech Republic joined NATO in 1999. Boris Yeltsin and his cabinet protested but were not really in a position to argue. Post-revolutionary Russia was in the throes of deprivation: the economic collapse due to Gorbachev's misconceived perestroika coupled with the inevitable hardship of a socialism-to-capitalism transition had resulted in an ineffectual and highly exploitative economy run by oligarchs and organized-crime dons, all but indistinguishable from one another. The price of oil was so low that it had stopped being a substantial revenue source. If Russia was to stay afloat, it needed American money, and therefore Bill Clinton's friendship.[21]

In May 1998, Thomas Friedman wrote in the *New York Times:* "There is one thing future historians will surely remark upon, and that is the utter poverty of imagination that characterized U.S. foreign policy in the late 1990s. They will note that one of the seminal events of this century took place between 1989 and 1992—the collapse of the Soviet Empire, which had the capability, imperial intentions and ideology to truly threaten the entire free world. . . . And what was America's response? It was to expand the NATO cold-war alliance against Russia and bring it closer to Russia's borders."[22]

The Clinton administration also aggravated Russian insecurities with its global military interventions. In Russians' eyes, no case epitomized this brazen geopolitical engineering more strongly than Kosovo.

In Yugoslavia, Kosovo was an autonomous province within Serbia. The idea behind the autonomy was to acknowledge the rights of a minority, Albanians, who shared the region with Serbs. Together with the rest of the mini-empire of Yugoslavia, in the 1980s Kosovo descended into ethnic strife. By 1998, clashes had grown into war between Albanians' Kosovo Liberation Army and Kosovo Serbs' paramilitary units. The president of Yugoslavia, Slobodan Milošević, sent in federal troops—not for peacekeeping, but to crush the Albanian rebels in the most brutal way. Milošević rejected all the United Nations resolutions of protest, explaining that Kosovo was an integral part of Serbia and that he would not consider Albanian rebels anything but terrorists.[23]

NATO countries, led by the United States, wanted to use military strikes against Serbia to prevent a humanitarian catastrophe. Russia expressed outrage. In the words of Strobe Talbott, Clinton's Russia adviser (and an avid supporter of a NATO military campaign against Serbia), Kosovo became the "substantiation of all the Russians' reasons for fearing NATO and opposing its expansion."[24]

Another great power with several potential Kosovos on its territory, China, also vehemently objected to any military campaign. Russia's and China's objections meant that the U.N. Security Council could not pass a resolution authorizing "humanitarian" intervention in Serbia. So NATO went in unilaterally. To use Madeleine Albright's language, that was a new, post–Cold War "common endeavor."

By doing so, the alliance was taking on an entirely new function, that of a policeman on a foreign territory not even bordering any NATO country. As the British author Geoffrey Wheatcroft wrote: "Whether or not a military response in the former Yugoslavia was desirable, it's hard to see what it had to do with NATO. Under the crucial Article 5 of the 1949 treaty [that created the alliance], the members agreed that 'an armed attack against one or more of them in Europe or North America shall be considered an attack against them all,' and whatever else Milošević and [Bosnian Serb army chief Ratko] Mladić might be accused of, they had not attacked any NATO member."[25]

Still furious, but willing to cooperate with NATO in order to play at least a limited role in the Balkans, Russia agreed to send peacekeeping troops to Kosovo. The uneasy partnership led to a brief all-out war scare. One day, Russian peacekeepers were found in a place they were not supposed to be, and the commander of

NATO forces in Kosovo, General Wesley Clark of the United States, ordered his British subordinate General Mike Jackson to attack and "overpower" them. Jackson famously told Clark off: "Sir, I am not going to start World War III for you."[26]

If for the NATO powers the intervention in Kosovo was a straightforward matter of rescuing the Kosovar people from a murderous Serbian regime—and for the United States in particular, an effort to prevent in Kosovo the genocide it had conspicuously failed to prevent a few years earlier in Rwanda—for other nations the matter was more complicated. When Kosovo proclaimed its independence from Serbia in 2008, many U.N. members objected. As of 2016, Kosovo had been recognized by 108 states, but among those that still ignored its existence were the powerhouses of the developing world—Russia, Argentina, Brazil, China, India, Iran, Mexico, and Singapore—as well as several U.S. allies, including Greece, Israel, Romania, Slovakia, and Spain. All of these states contained minorities striving for nationhood that might be inspired by Kosovo's example to try to cleave off chunks of territory and declare independence. One of the nations objecting to Kosovo's recognition was Ukraine. If American diplomacy remained blissfully unaware that by crafting an independent Kosovo it had opened a Pandora's box, politicians in Kiev knew very well that they had their own potential Kosovo in Crimea.

As edited by Western advisers, the declaration of Kosovo independence emphasized that Kosovo was a special case, not a precedent to be exploited by secessionists worldwide. Yet as Timothy Garton Ash pointed out, all sixty-eight other members of the Unrepresented Nations and Peoples Organization, "from Abkhazia to Zanzibar," were "special cases too." The "Kosovo precedent" became a rallying cry in every separatist hotbed: Nagorno-Karabakh and Trans-Dniester in the former Soviet Union; the Basque Country and Catalonia in Europe; Northern Cyprus; Quebec.[27]

The enthusiastic American support of the breakaway republic had prompted Russians to take the attitude, "if they can do it, so should we." After a brief war with Georgia in 2008, Russia sponsored "sovereignty and independence" for the Georgian provinces of Abkhazia and South Ossetia.[28]

On George W. Bush's watch, NATO membership was extended to Bulgaria, Romania, Slovakia, Slovenia, Albania, Croatia, and three post-Soviet countries—Latvia, Lithuania, and Estonia. U.S.-Russia relations plummeted. But bigger challenges were to come: the candidacies of both Ukraine and Georgia for admission to NATO.

By Russians' lights, *this* crossed the line. As a British author put it, Washington would have felt the same had Leonid Brezhnev "invited Mexico and Cuba to join the Warsaw Pact."[29]

Regime Change in a Foreign Country

Since the end of the Cold War, supposedly won by the United States, the winner has scored remarkably few foreign policy victories. No doubt many factors had contributed to the debacles in Iraq, Libya, and elsewhere, but one major miscalculation seems to have been the striking readiness to launch political engineering and sometimes endorse regime change in countries that are neither willing nor ready to ally with the West.

The moral permissibility of such interference aside, typically neither the U.S.-sponsored opposition nor the U.S. representatives engineering the transition of power have a positive program in mind. The "down with" bit is the easiest part of any uprising, but if there is no clear answer to the "what next" question, in all likelihood all the sacrifice would be in vain.

In 2004, in the viciously contested presidential elections in Ukraine, the United States supported the "pro-Western" candidate, Viktor Yushchenko, as Moscow rallied behind the "pro-Russian" Viktor

Yanukovych. The campaign was nothing short of operatic. A dig in Yanukovych's dirty linen revealed felony: as a young man, he had been found guilty of violent street crime. Now he professed to be "reformed," a claim that many did not find entirely convincing. His opponent, Viktor Yushchenko, a very handsome man, had suddenly developed a brutal rash on his face. He claimed poisoning, and blood tests run by a European clinic confirmed the presence of herbicide, dioxin. Blaming the Russian secret services for his Shrek looks, Yushchenko bravely went on campaigning.

The "pro-Russian" Yanukovych claimed electoral victory, but the many reports of fraud coming from polling stations around the country caused popular anger, and that led to riots. Yushchenko refused to concede; as his campaign had been using the color orange for banners, t-shirts, and other paraphernalia, the resistance was dubbed the "Orange Revolution." The movement got the support of the U.S. government, but the Kremlin, mistaking American cheerleading for a disciplined cabal, exaggerated the level of U.S. involvement. Much was made of the fact that Yushchenko's wife was an American citizen and a former U.S. State Department official.[30]

Under pressure, a Ukrainian court annulled the results and ordered a rerun. The schism within Ukrainian society remained so strong that even after the electoral fraud scandal, 44 percent of Ukrainians voted for the disgraced Yanukovych.

With 52 percent of the vote, Yushchenko's victory was secure, but the Orange Revolution was not. Yushchenko's presidency was defined by infighting, corruption, abuse of executive power, and ineffectiveness. Running for reelection in 2010, he got less than 6 percent of the popular vote. But Washington's encouragement of the Orange Revolution had convinced the Kremlin that the U.S. was capable of unseating a government in the post-Soviet space. That was a game changer.[31]

To judge from its record of intervention in non-Western societies in the past twenty-five years, America's urge to improve the world has become persistent, aggressive, and unyielding. Bill Clinton had called the United States the "indispensable nation," and Barack Obama called it "exceptional." Despite the fact that Obama's declaration was largely for domestic consumption, intended to appease conservative audiences in the United States, Vladimir Putin responded with a furious piece on the op-ed page of the *New York Times*. "God created us equal," he growled. "It is extremely dangerous to encourage people to see themselves as exceptional, whatever the motivation. . . . It is alarming that military intervention in internal conflicts in foreign countries has become commonplace for the United States." The interventionist intellectual Robert Kagan responded with a smile: "What gives the United States the right to act on behalf of a liberal world order? In truth, nothing does, nothing beyond the conviction that the liberal world order is the most just."[32]

Where Putin saw geopolitical failure—Afghanistan "reeling," Libya "divided into tribes and clans," Iraq still in the throes of civil war—Kagan saw promising if unfinished political engineering. Most of the "sizeable" U.S. military operations of the past twenty years, he noted with approval, had not been responses to "perceived threats to vital national interests. All aimed at defending and extending the liberal world order—by toppling dictators, reversing coups, and attempting to restore democracies."[33]

The interventionist politician most eager to seize the opportunity for another Kitchen Debate was Senator John McCain. Who is Putin to judge the United States, McCain indignantly asked in an essay posted on the Russian news site *Pravda*. "He has given you a political system that is sustained by corruption and repression and isn't strong enough to tolerate dissent." He had made Russia a "friend to tyrants and an enemy to the oppressed"; he did not even have enough faith in the Russian people to trust them to handle freedom. "I do believe in you," McCain assured his Russian audience. "I believe in your capacity for self-government and your desire for justice and opportunity." Exemplary in its tone deafness—McCain was talking to a foreign nation as one would to a delinquent child—the address became infamous.[34]

Furthermore, no term McCain used—"justice," "opportunity," "freedom"—could be defined with any degree of precision. Twenty-first-century Americans do not see eye to eye on fundamental rights and liberties, and while debating these fundamentals is, of course, the norm of human existence, it is strange to demand that "they" be like "us" when "we" cannot agree on what we are. Why, for example, advocate gay marriage in developing countries at a time when homophobia was rampant among American presidential hopefuls?

What McCain no doubt viewed as a plain-spoken expression of universal values that only barbarians would oppose, Russians saw as an example of arrogant, almost willful cognitive dissonance. When it came to American support of the Russian punk group Pussy Riot, the dissonance came to seem grotesque.

In 2010, the members of Pussy Riot staged a flash mob performance in the national cathedral in Moscow, chanting "Mother of God, kick Putin out." It is most unlikely that the action was intrinsically political: the group's prior performances had included copulation in a natural history museum. The event was more in the vein of Marina Abramović's artistic provocation than Andrei Sakharov's ideological dissent. No matter how we define it, however, it involved the desecration of a holy site.

Rather stupidly, a Moscow court sentenced the young women to jail terms. But when commentators in the United States declared Pussy Riot martyrs of the anti-Putin revolutionary movement, many Russians found it odd: they had not forgotten that just thirty years before, the privileges of Russian Christians had sat at the top of Washington's human rights agenda. In the days of Jimmy Carter and Ronald Reagan, desecration of a church in Russia would have been called a godless Communist act. Yet on the day the 2014 Olympics opened in Sochi, Russia, the *New York Times* ran an editorial stating that no celebration of Russian Olympic hospitality should overshadow the plight of the women of Pussy Riot. Americans saw no contradiction: they had spoken out for freedom of religion for Russian Christians when that was under assault, and they spoke out for Pussy Riot's freedom of expression for the same reason—even if that expression offended the very Christians they had once supported.[35]

But Russians did see a contradiction, and to them it smelled of opportunism. Washington seemed willing to support *any* dissent in Russia—pro-church under Communism, anti-church under Putin—so long as it undermined existing authority. If the Western campaign of solidarity with the women of Pussy Riot had any practical effect at all, it was to compromise the opposition in the eyes of the pro-Putin Russian majority.

Obama's ambassador to Moscow, Michael McFaul, certainly did not see it that way. He had come up with the concept of a "dual track" in Russia: dealing simultaneously with the government *and* the opposition. Arriving to Moscow in January 2012, he cheerfully introduced himself to the Russian media as a "specialist on democracy and revolution." The timing could not have been worse: Moscow was going through the strongest anti-Putin protests ever. McFaul apparently thought he had arrived just in time for the start of the Russian Spring.

The Kremlin did not hesitate to make its displeasure clear. Harassed by government TV crews, who seemed to know the ambassador's schedule better than his assistants did and shadowed his every move, McFaul eventually lost his cool, publicly called Russia a "barbaric, uncivilized country," and in February 2014 angrily submitted his resignation—in the midst of the crisis his "dual track" diplomacy had facilitated.

Twenty years earlier, the then "pro-Western" Russian foreign minister Andrei Kozyrev told Clinton's Russia hand Strobe Talbott: "It's bad enough having you people tell us what you're going to do whether we like it or not. Don't add insult to injury by also telling us that it's *in our interests* to obey your orders." Talbott's assistant at the time, Victoria Nuland, good-naturedly commented: "That's what happens when you try to get the Russians to eat their spinach. The more you tell them it's good for them, the more they gag." In his memoir, Talbott smirks: "Among those of us working on Russia policy, 'administering the spinach treatment' became shorthand for one of our principal activities in the years that followed."[36]

When, at the end of the spinach years, Russia handed a landslide electoral victory to the xenophobic strongman Vladimir Putin, Talbott and Clinton acted surprised. Nuland, meanwhile, moved up in the world, making a name for herself in December 2013 on the streets of the Ukrainian capital, Kiev.

TWO

Protagonists

Every person who has ever crossed from Russia into Ukraine on land—and until recently that was how most travelers did it—must have noticed a gradual change in the scenery occurring in the borderland. No natural boundary separates Ukraine from Russia, no mountain range or river, and the terrain the traveler negotiates stays the same—a treeless plain, occasionally made unattractive by overdevelopment—yet something changes, and at some point, still in Russia or already in Ukraine, the traveler is aware of having entered a different culture. The front yards have flowers, if not exactly flower gardens. Logs and brick give way to whitewashed walls. Streets are cleaner, the people louder and more cheery.

From a junction in central Ukraine—say Kharkiv, or Zaporizhia—you have a choice of continuing south or west. If you go west, aiming at Galicia with Lviv its capital city, you will encounter yet another cultural metamorphosis, perhaps best represented by the presence of Catholic churches, which the locals still call by their Polish name, *kostyol*. Continue west, and you arrive at one of the border crossings—into Poland, Slovakia, Hungary, or Romania. This would be Europe's edge.

But if you have chosen the southern route, toward the Black Sea and the Sea of Azov, instead of the Occident you would be traveling toward the Orient, its approach announced by the Turkic names of hamlets, creeks, and junctions. When translated, these names speak of abandonment, war, and drought. You are on what used to be called the Wild Fields. The Crimean Peninsula dangles from their underbelly.

Ukraine-Russia

When Moscow and the European powers clashed in Ukraine in the twenty-first century, the catastrophe continued a historical pattern. Theoretically, Ukraine's sheer size should have prevented such a staggering loss of agency, but paradoxically, one could argue that for Ukraine, its size was its worst enemy: too much diversity, and too little time to bind it all together. Western Lviv thought of itself as Europe, eastern Donbass identified with Russia, and the rest of the country struggled between these extremes. Centuries of imperial rule by Austria, Poland, Russia, and Turkey left it in fragments.

The underlying reason for the Ukraine-Russia conflict is that both are offshoots of the same long-dead state: siblings with very different fortunes. One became an empire, another a borderland. It is hard to find another example of this kind of connection: Russia and Ukraine are joined more tightly than England and Scotland or the United States and Canada.

The first state of the eastern Slavs developed on the upper Dnieper River in the 880s. It is remembered as Kievan Rus'. A millennium later, Kiev is the capital of Ukraine; in Russian tradition, it remains the "Mother of All Russian Cities." Ivan the Terrible of Russia claimed to be a direct descendant of the Kievan dynasty.[1]

Seeking unity for the loosely connected assembly of tribes and princelings, the princes of Kiev implemented a cultural revolution by borrowing Eastern Orthodox Christianity from Byzantium and then enforcing it as a state religion. The Cyrillic alphabet came from Byzantium as well. The idea was brilliant: the enforcement of borrowed memes put all subjects of the Kievan prince in an equal position. In the ecclesiastical writings and folklore of Rus', this Kievan revolution is a focal point—not a mere episode in the nation's history but its beginning. With their common language, alphabet, faith, early statehood, and the pantheon of saints and heroes, Russians and Ukrainians share a national creation myth.[2]

Not unlike other early states, Rus' quickly disintegrated. The hundred years from 1146 to 1246 saw forty-seven changes of head of state, involving twenty-four different princes. The Mongol invasion of the thirteenth century hit Rus' at the height of disunity, making the Mongols' victory instantaneous and its consequences lasting. As a Russian chronicle stated in 1224, "for our sins, there came unknown tribes. No one knew who they were or what was their origin, faith, or tongue," but they had already "conquered many lands."[3]

The southern principalities of Rus' sitting at the edge of the steppe (a natural avenue for Mongol cavalry)—Kiev, Galich, Chernigov—were devastated, but the northern Russians hung on in the dense boreal forests of Vladimir and Novgorod. By 1300, the surviving Kievan elites, including the leaders of the Orthodox Church, had moved north. The south entered seven centuries of statelessness; the north eventually grew into what is nowadays known as Russia.[4]

The name "Ukraine," meaning "borderland," initially meant the periphery of Kiev but gradually became the name for all the southern territories of the former Rus'. That was what the area had become geopolitically—contested land for Ottomans, Russians, and Poles.[5]

In the sixteenth century, most of Ukraine fell under Polish rule. Its upper class adopted the language and culture of the conqueror (the process known as Polonization), causing a critical alienation between the elites and the lower classes. When Bohdan Khmelnytsky led Ukrainian peasants in a revolt against the Poles in 1648, he was also fighting his own country's aristocracy. Though a hero to Ukrainians, Khmelnytsky became infamous among Jews for the exceptional brutality of the Cossack pogroms under his rule.

Seeing the impossibility of domestic consensus, Khmelnytsky realized that he needed a powerful foreign patron and that his options were limited to just Russia and the Crimean Khanate, an offshoot of the Mongol empire, and by this time a protectorate of the Ottomans.

Russia was Poland's nemesis. Russians were Eastern Orthodox, like the majority of Ukrainians. There was little doubt, though, that eventually the Kremlin would want total control over Ukraine. But no lasting alliance with the only alternative patron, the Crimean Khanate, was possible, as Khmelnytsky had a chance to see for himself after visiting its capital, Bakhchisaray: there was nothing in it for the khan. Choosing what looked a lesser evil, in 1654 Khmelnytsky pledged allegiance to the Russian tsar.[6]

For nearly four hundred years since then, Russians have celebrated the 1654 pledge as a "reunification" of the "two Slavic peoples." That was not how Khmelnytsky intended it, but with his death his nation-building project fell apart. The succession crisis led to a fratricidal war commanded by regional warlords, who were, in turn, manipulated by foreigners: Russians, Poles, Ottomans, Tatars, and Swedes. In Ukraine, the period is still remembered till this day as the Ruin (*Ruina*).

By the time of Khmelnytsky's death, with opportunism as their modus operandi, the upper classes of eastern and central Ukraine sided with Russia. Polonization was replaced by Russification, which lasted as long as the aristocracy did. The greatest Ukrainian man of letters, the nineteenth-century satirist Nikolai Gogol, wrote in Russian.[7]

In the eighteenth century, Russia's war against the Ottoman Empire and its client state, the Crimean Khanate, did not seem to directly concern Ukraine. The Turkic-speaking khanate, which at that time encompassed not just the Crimean peninsula but the Wild Fields and the entire region surrounding the Sea of Azov, was next door but not part of the Ukrainian narrative. This changed when Russia took over the khanate, christened the region "Novorossiya," or New Russia, and began to rule it straight from the imperial capital as frontier provinces. Trade hubs and industrial centers along the coasts, from Odessa to Taganrog, were multinational. So was the new farming class.[8]

In the official vernacular of the empire, Ukraine became "Malorossia"—"Little Russia" (Belorussia, now Belarus, was "White Russia," and the imperial Russian core "Velikorossia," or "Greater Russia"). The basic administrative imperial unit was the province (*guberniya*); no entity called Ukraine appeared on any map. The idea of Ukrainian nationhood would not appear until the mid–nineteenth century.[9]

This idea was conceived in Ukraine's western regions, collectively known as Galicia and belonging to Austria-Hungary. While hardly a paragon of free thinking, the Habsburg Empire was nevertheless more liberal than the Romanov dynasty in Russia. In the words of the historian Orest Subtelny, Galicia became the "bastion of Ukrainianism."[10] Many believe it still is.

The task of defining, or, to use Benedict Anderson's term, "imagining," Ukraine was similar to that facing a number of Eastern European peoples, all of whom were influenced by the new German concept of nationhood—common language and shared heroic mythology. A founding father of nationalism in Ukraine, Mykhailo Hrushevsky (1866–1934), dismissed the political and cultural fragmentation of the previous six centuries as inconsequential, claiming that since the breakup of the Kievan state Ukrainians had still continued as a single ethnos, or nation. Looking for a historical myth that would separate Ukrainians from Russians, nationalists zoomed in on Cossacks, denizens of an autonomous rogue republic, Bohdan Khmelnytsky one of them. This mythology, however, held little appeal for the Russian and Jewish artisans and bourgeoisie who made up the majorities in Ukrainian cities, and who saw little benefit in participating in a new imagined community, particularly since the myth of "Cossackdom" was intensely xenophobic. The national poet of Ukraine, Taras Shevchenko (1814–1861), who wrote Cossacks into the literary canon, defined them by their struggles against "Polaks" (*lyahi*), "Ivans" (*moskaly*), "kikes" (*zhidy*), and Tatar "infidels" (*pohantsy*).[11]

Ukraine had no clear boundaries, either in reality or in collective memory. Mental maps of the country differed widely depending on who was thinking them up, and when, and where. Crimea was not part of any "mental map." Nationalist lore remembered it as an infidel horde that raided Ukraine in search of slaves and loot; liberal intelligentsia such as the outstanding poet Larysa Kosach-Kvitka (1871–1913), known by her nom de plume Lesya Ukrainka, empathized with Tatars as victims of Russian imperialism, on par with Ukrainians themselves.[12]

For Ukraine, only a catalyst of extraordinary proportions could have made a national movement possible. It arrived in the form of the two Russian revolutions of 1917. The revolution of February swept away the Romanov monarchy, and the revolution of October took care of pretty much everything else, leaving no value in the country standing and hardly any structures. The civil war, apocalyptic in brutality, continued for three years. Finland, Estonia, Latvia, and Lithuania used the chaos to secede: each was a compact territory where the educated class upheld a national myth. Ukraine, still fragmented, tried and failed.

Having no structure, power base, or resources, the succession of three nationalist regimes in Kiev between November 1917 and December 1919 (the Central Rada, the Hetmanate, and the Directory) exercised suzerainty only over Kiev. Throughout 1918, Ukraine was occupied by Germany, a condition incompatible with any but titular independence. After signing the armistice in the west in November 1918, the Germans evacuated, and the only force holding Ukraine together departed with them. Total collapse and lawlessness followed. No government could claim continuous authority. In two years, Kiev changed hands eighteen times.[13]

The very notion of the "territory of Ukraine" remained unresolved. The Paris Peace Conference of 1919 refused to recognize it as a state. Woodrow Wilson was a strong proponent of a revived Poland but entertained no such ideas about Ukraine. The revived Poland, meanwhile, occupied Galicia in the spring of 1919 and received the allied powers' blessing.[14]

It is ironic that bringing down statues of Lenin became a mark of the civil conflict in Ukraine in 2013–2016, because Lenin is the person who put Ukraine on the political map. Under Soviet rule, the Ukrainian Soviet Socialist Republic was endowed with all the attributes of a state.

When the Union of Soviet Socialist Republics was in the works in the fall of 1922, Lenin was a dying man. A succession of strokes, striking at an early age (he turned fifty-two that year), bestowed bitter lucidity upon him. The state he was leaving behind was terribly unfair, and the person likely to succeed him, Joseph Stalin, was certain to make it even more repressive. The principles of the Union became Lenin's last battle. Stalin wanted minorities in the USSR to have cultural autonomy—meaning just titular recognition of ethnic diversity. Lenin wanted the larger ethnicities to have quasi-states with all the attributes of sovereignty, including maintaining their own borders with the outside world—the latter was a provision Lenin insisted on, in case a republic chose to secede.[15]

Within a few years, Ukraine had established itself as second among equals in the USSR, after Russia proper. In 1945, at Stalin's insistence, the United States accepted the Ukrainian Soviet Socialist Republic as a founding member of the United Nations—a bizarre arrangement legitimizing Ukraine's ersatz sovereignty (the only other faux state among the U.N. founding members was another Slavic Soviet republic, Belorussia).

Having Polonized with the Poles and Russified with the Russians, in the Soviet Union the Ukrainian elites Sovietized. Together with Russians, Ukrainians made up the bulk of the Communist Party, KGB, police, and officer corps. The leader of the USSR between 1964 and 1982, Leonid Brezhnev, came from Ukraine, as did several other Politburo members.[16]

No other republic of the union increased its territory as much as Ukraine did. In 1939, after dividing up Poland with Hitler, Stalin assigned Galicia to the Ukrainian SSR. Ukraine now encompassed both former Russian and former Polish territories. In 1954, Nikita Khrushchev awarded it Crimea. As Orest Subtelny noted, because Crimea was the "historic homeland of the Crimean Tatars," the Russians did not have "the moral right to give it away nor did the Ukrainians have the right to accept it."[17]

Lenin's 1922 provisions paved the way for the bloodless disintegration of the USSR in 1991: the republics had a right to secede, and the fact that each had a border with the outside world facilitated this. Ukraine seceded from the union with most structures of statehood already in place—ministries, law enforcement, schools, research centers, power grid, transportation system, even a modest foreign service. The military had to be reorganized, but not forged anew: Ukraine had inherited the Soviet Union's well-trained officer corps, infrastructure, and arsenals.

But tensions among different regions, frozen by the federal Soviet state for decades, now surfaced. As in Russia, the post-Soviet transition to a free market economy led to the emergence of an exploitative class of the shady new rich, presided over by the oligarchs—fifty people owning about 85 percent of national wealth. Their business empires tended to be region-based, contributing to general fragmentation. Times were especially hard in eastern and southern Ukraine: that's where the Soviet-era megalomaniac industry enterprises, now unfit for the new economy, were. Already in the early 1990s, thoughtful observers, of which Ambassador Jack F. Matlock was one, "began to wonder if Ukraine could retain its unity if the process of regional estrangement continued."[18]

Ukrainian politics became incredibly volatile. In the 2012 parliamentary elections, the party of the hero of the Orange Revolution in 2004, Viktor Yushchenko, received barely more than 1 percent of the vote. Riches to rags has been the fate of many a politician, but the Ukrainian seesaw suggests an electorate entirely divorced from the political machine, feeling no loyalty to and, for sure, no trust for any political force. Political parties are the dayflies of Ukrainian politics, set up by a leader on the eve of general vote, only to crumble after serving the campaign's purposes. Almost twenty-five years since independence, Ukraine's multiparty system remains tentative and unstable. This instability is a direct outgrowth of the country's historical lack of definition.

In *The Clash of Civilizations*, Samuel P. Huntington defined Ukraine as "cleft" and Russia as "torn." "Torn" countries, Huntington argued, were the ones struggling with their civilizational belonging; "cleft" nations had large groups clearly belonging to "different civilizations." Ukraine, in Huntington's view, was a "cleft country with two distinct cultures," the "civilizational fault line between the West and Orthodoxy" running through Ukraine's "heart."

Huntington's analysis seems to govern American experts' current interpretation of the crisis. But the assumption that Ukraine is divided only along east-west lines is a damaging approximation. In Ukraine, divisions cross neighborhoods and families, not only regions. In Huntington's terminology, Ukraine is at least as "torn" as Russia is.[19]

The Black Sea Fleet and Sevastopol

The Soviet Union was dismantled with frightening ease and staggering thoughtlessness. Among other things, no provisions were made for the reapportioning of federal property, including the Black Sea Fleet and its facilities.[20]

The USSR ran twenty-six naval bases on the Black Sea. On twenty-two of them, Russian sailors went to sleep on December 24, 1991, in the Soviet Union and woke up the next morning in a foreign country. Nineteen bases were in Ukraine, three in the Republic of Georgia. The facilities in Georgia, such as Poti and Batumi, were second-tier. Ukraine had gotten the best.[21]

The only Black Sea port left in Russian hands was Novorossiisk (close to Sochi). Due to "adverse weather conditions," mainly local storms from the northeast called *bora* (from Boreas, the Greek god of the north wind), Novorossiisk remains closed on average for two months a year. Hitting the area in fall and winter, the *bora* brings winds exceeding one hundred miles per hour, turning the harbor into a boiling cauldron and tossing smaller vessels ashore like toys. After a *bora* sank a Russian fleet in 1848, the Admiralty prohibited the navy from anchoring in Novorossiisk between November and March. The British navy's manual warned that Novorossiisk was "very dangerous, on account of N.E. winds, which are prevalent from the month of September to the beginning of April; it sometimes blows with the fury of a hurricane," rushing down from the mountains "with such violence, and causing such a sea, that vessels are driven on shore."[22]

It is simply not possible to run a big operational facility in Novorossiisk. If Russia was to keep a substantial naval force on the Black Sea, it had no alternative to Sevastopol. This is why the "Crimean question" came up on Russia's official agenda just one month after the collapse of the USSR. In January 1992, the Russian parliament's committee on foreign affairs proposed declaring Khrushchev's 1954 act granting Crimea to Ukraine "invalid and devoid of legal force." The motion was dismissed by Yeltsin, who considered it too aggressive. Negotiations started. It took five years to prepare the Partition Treaty on the Status and Conditions of the Black Sea Fleet. Signed on May 28, 1997, the treaty allowed for the armaments and bases to be shared by two independent fleets. Russia could lease Sevastopol and other naval facilities in Crimea for ten more years. In addition, it could keep up to 25,000 soldiers, 132 armored vehicles, and 22 airplanes on the peninsula. In 2010, the arrangement was extended until 2042—in exchange for discounted natural gas supplies to Kiev.[23]

A British Russia expert, Angus Roxburgh, calls the price Russia paid for the Crimean bases "extortionate." In a book published in 2013 he quotes Vladimir Putin, who clearly agreed: "'The price we are now asked to pay is out of this world. . . . No military base in the world costs that much. Prices like that simply do not exist. If we look at what the contract would cost us over ten years, it amounts to $40–45 billion.'"[24]

As often happens, the treaty did not resolve the underlying conflict.

Petrostate

The term frequently used to describe Russia nowadays—"petrostate"—was popularized by Marshall Goldman. In the book of that title, Goldman, who had been watching the Kremlin for five decades, noted with grudging admiration how Putin seemed to be winning the "giant chess match" of energy politics.[25]

Vladimir Putin had appeared, seemingly from nowhere, in 1999. The first foreign leader to be told of his appointment as prime minister of Russia, Israeli prime minister Ehud Barak, reported it this way to Bill Clinton: "The replacement that was mentioned to me was some guy whose name is Putin." Russians shared his bewilderment. On the day Yeltsin introduced Putin as his designated successor, few Muscovites knew who he was. When interviewed, they referred to the new leader of the country as someone whose name "started with a P."[26]

Putin's eventual popularity with the Russian Main Street came from two sources. One was his claim to limit the power of the oligarchs, kick them out of politics, and restore Russia's "vertical of power," a euphemism for strong state. Another was completely accidental. During the Yeltsin years, the price of crude oil on world markets had fallen as low as $10 a barrel, sending the newly independent Russian nation into bankruptcy. In Putin's first year in office, the price of crude skyrocketed, filling the coffers of the state treasury and allowing many government offices that had become almost moribund for lack of funds to begin functioning again. Putin was able to claim credit for reviving the state, government workers were once again being paid, and money trickled down to the people. Russia paid off the last of its foreign debt in 2006, and in 2008, when crude oil crossed $100 a barrel, it could boast almost $800 billion in foreign reserves.[27] As Stephen Weisman noted in the *New York Times* in 2006, a "more assertive Russia" was back, and the United States was not "welcome to set up shop in the old Soviet empire."[28]

In 2015, Russia's energy exports to Europe netted $160 billion a year, and Europe depended on Russia for at least 30 percent of its natural gas needs. According to a March 2014 estimate, Russian oil and gas made up 98 percent of all energy imports in Slovakia, 92 percent in Lithuania, 91 percent in Poland, 90 percent in Bulgaria,

86 percent in Hungary, 76 percent in Finland, 73 percent in the Czech Republic, 72 percent in Latvia, 69 percent in Estonia, and 47 percent in Romania. All of these nations were once either part of the Soviet Union or in its zone of influence. But Western Europe had grown dependent on Russian energy as well. Sweden got 46 percent of its energy imports from Russia, Greece 40 percent, the Netherlands 34 percent, Germany and Belgium 30 percent, Italy 28 percent, and France 17 percent.[29]

In his fourteen years in the Kremlin, Putin has cultivated and increased this dependence, using it to forge special relationships with a number of European customers, especially Germany and Italy. The only problem for him was Ukraine: about 50 percent of Russian gas flows to Europe through its territory. In the past the service had been disrupted several times: Moscow and Kiev could not agree on a fair selling price for Ukrainian purchases, though it must be noted that until 2005 Russia sold gas to Ukraine at a heavily discounted rate. The resulting annual subsidy to the Ukrainian economy amounted to at least $3 billion a year—a price Putin was willing to pay to keep Kiev in Moscow's orbit. Whenever Russia stopped supplies to Kiev, Ukrainians started siphoning gas contractually designated for Europe. Alienating European customers was not part of the plan, and Putin decided a bypass was needed.

In 2005, Putin and German chancellor Gerhard Schröder concluded a deal for Nord Stream, an offshore mega-pipeline in the Baltic Sea. All of the other Baltic nations—Sweden, Poland, Lithuania, Latvia, Estonia—protested, but Germany paid no attention. The bypass became operational in 2011, and after Schröder stepped down as chancellor of Germany, he became the chairman of the board of Nord Stream A.G.[30]

Nord Stream eased but did not solve the problem of gas transit through Ukraine. Its capacity was still not enough to make the Ukrainian route redundant, and in any case it did nothing for southern Europe. Putin started negotiating to create a *South* Stream, which would connect Russia and the Balkans. Once it became operational, Russian gas exports to Europe would be immune to any crisis in Ukraine. Coupled with Nord Stream, the two would become Russia's pincers holding on to Europe.

Pushing the project forward is Gazprom, the giant Russian energy company, with foreign partners that include Eni of Italy, Wintershall of Germany, and Electricité de France (EDF). Austria, Bulgaria, Croatia, Greece, Hungary, and Slovenia have all made intergovernmental agreements with Russia facilitating the deal.

As this one example demonstrates, the Russia-Ukraine relationship is staggeringly complex. The two countries, their populations, culture, history, and economy are so interconnected that they may be called the conjoined twins of the Slavic world.

One would have thought that on a space like that, great powers would tread carefully. But no such luck.

THREE

A Chain of Unfortunate Events

It will probably never be known with certainty what exactly happened in Kiev in the winter of 2013–2014. Not that information was scarce, but the opposite: there has been too much of it. The sheer number of conflicting uncorroborated sources used by political parties, governments, and media was dumbfounding, and as every digital source—video, photograph, tweet—claimed authenticity and immediacy, it was virtually impossible to resolve conflicts between different angles, perspectives, and tags. When every picture can be invisibly doctored, none can be trusted.

If the warring parties could agree on any interpretation at all, that would be a bare-bones narrative: in the fall of 2013, Ukraine was poised to choose between two economic patrons—Russia and the European Union. Contrary to the wishes of many, the president of Ukraine, Viktor Yanukovych, chose Russia; protests started in Kiev; there were clashes between rioters and government forces, and people on both sides died; Yanukovych fled, and opposition leaders formed a pro-E.U. revolutionary government. Beyond that utterly minimal summary, accord ends.

Euromaidan

Elected to the Ukrainian presidency in 2010, the "pro-Russian" Yanukovych was not averse to dallying with the West, and once in office, he continued the precarious East-West "dual vector" balancing act of his predecessors. His cabinet dropped plans to join NATO, but not the intention to intensify cooperation with the European Union.[1]

The Ukraine–European Union Association Agreement was conceived in 2012. The majority in the Ukrainian Rada (its parliament), including Yanukovych's party, supported the move. The agreement was to be signed at the E.U. summit on November 29, 2013, in the Lithuanian capital of Vilnius.

At first, Putin applied the stick. In August, Russia changed its customs regulations for Ukrainian goods, causing a 10 percent drop in Ukrainian exports—a hard blow for an already destitute country. But that alone did not deter Yanukovych. What made him change his mind were the finalized figures of Western aid, presented in November. The European Union offered $838 million in loans; the International Monetary Fund $4 billion, provided Yanukovych made budget cuts and raised domestic gas prices by 40 percent. Putin responded with a promise of $15 billion in loans plus $3 billion a year in natural-gas subsidies. On November 21, Yanukovych's cabinet suspended its deal with the European Union.

An overlooked fact is that no one ever actually offered Ukraine *membership* in the European Union. Contrary to the beliefs of the pro-E.U. Ukrainians, the "association" would not have given them the rights of unrestricted travel and access to jobs throughout the continent enjoyed by citizens of E.U. nations. For Brussels, the underlying rationale for expanding to Ukraine was to take over a market with 44 million customers. At the same time, Ukrainian agricultural produce, while popular in Russia, did not stand a chance in the heavily regulated European markets. Still, indignant that Yanukovych had made the strategic decision unilaterally, protestors filled the government quarter of Kiev's Right Bank, along Mykhailo Hrushevsky and Instytutska streets. The largest crowds assembled on Maidan Nezalezhnosti—Independence Square. As the protestors demanded association with the European Union, the movement was dubbed the Euromaidan.

Various sources, referencing different dates, estimated the number of participants anywhere from 50,000 to 800,000. More than half were from western Ukraine.

They were quickly joined by far-right groups vowing to persecute "Ivans and kikes." Putin's provocateurs stepped in as well. Rallies turned violent. What had started as a grassroots protest against a "rogue state" developed into something infinitely more complex: an interregional conflict informed by different ideologies, special interests, a shadow economy, and foreign intervention.[2]

From Kiev, clashes between revolutionaries and loyalists spread to the provinces. Government buildings were attacked, local administrations overtaken. The Euromaidan groups prevailed in the west, Russophiles in the east.

There is plenty of evidence to support the claim that during his years in power, Yanukovych enriched his own associates at the expense of other oligarchs. There is also evidence of the anti-Yanukovych oligarchs' deep involvement in the 2013–2014 political overhaul. Petro Poroshenko, known as the Chocolate King for having made his fortune as the owner of a confectionary manufacturer (and who would later become the president of Ukraine), boastfully admitted: "From the beginning, I was one of the organizers of the Maidan. My television channel—Channel 5—played a tremendously important role." Another oligarch, Dmitry Firtash, claimed to have manipulated both the Euromaidan *and* Poroshenko. And so on. The events in Kiev would not have been possible without the oligarchs' participation, but hardly any tycoon had a clear vision of where things should be going, and steered the protests accordingly.[3]

The same applies to the revolt's foreign participants.

Regime Change

If Yanukovych's was a rogue state, U.S. foreign policy in Ukraine in 2013–2014 can only be described as rogue diplomacy. Most certainly without the imprimatur of President Obama, and perhaps even without a silent nod from Secretary of State John Kerry, a group of senior American diplomats allied with bipartisan interventionists in Congress started brokering regime change in Kiev.

The protagonists included assistant secretary of state for European and Eurasian affairs Victoria Nuland, U.S. ambassador to Ukraine Geoffrey R. Pyatt, and Senator John McCain.

McCain was the first prominent American to descend on Kiev to fraternize with the people on the barricades and encourage them to overthrow the democratically elected president. On December 15, 2013, he told Ukrainians that their future was "with Europe," not Russia: "The free world is with you, America is with you, I am with you. Ukraine will make Europe better and Europe will make Ukraine better." Speaking to 200,000 rebels in a foreign capital, he said without apparent irony that he wanted to make it clear to "Russia and Vladimir Putin that interference in the affairs of Ukraine is not acceptable to the United States." What had started as competition over spheres of interest was, in McCain's telling, turning into a civilizational clash, the forces of light against the forces of darkness.[4]

Putin could have dismissed this fiery talk. McCain was a loose cannon and had been bashing Russia for years, at one point leading Putin to quip, tastelessly, "I don't blame McCain. He spent five years in a cage in Vietnam. Anyone would've lost his marbles there."[5] But interference by U.S. government officials was another matter.

Assistant secretary of state Nuland, the one who had coined the "spinach treatment" adage, seems to have been the spearhead of the project. Not insignificantly, her husband was the leading neoconservative intellectual Robert Kagan. During the crisis, Nuland was a frequent visitor to Kiev. In turmoil like that it was not humanly possible *not* to make mistakes, and on December 13, 2013, speaking to the U.S.-Ukraine Foundation Conference in Washington, Nuland revealed that since 1991, the United States had "invested over $5 billion to assist Ukraine" in building "democratic skills and institutions." She later claimed she was "still jetlagged" from her "third trip in five weeks to Ukraine," and maybe that's why the wording was dangerously imprecise, the message conflicted, the delivery most certainly untimely. In a subsequent interview, Nuland reluctantly confirmed that the United States had spent $5 billion "on supporting the aspirations of the Ukrainian people to have a strong, democratic government that represents their interests. But," she stressed, "we certainly didn't spend any money supporting the Maidan; that was a spontaneous movement."[6] It had been spontaneous—in the beginning.

If John McCain found Putin the personification of evil, Nuland became that for Russians. Later, the Russian foreign minister would say: "That woman has played a very nasty role at every stage of the crisis in Ukraine."[7]

Nuland first made headlines on December 11: visiting Independence Square in Kiev, she offered sandwiches to antigovernment protesters and police in front of the TV cameras. Taken as an intensely patronizing gesture, Nuland's sandwiches became infamous, and not only in Russia. When pressed by CNN's Christiane

Amanpour, Nuland explained that the "visit happened the night after the Ukrainian special forces . . . moved against peaceful demonstrators, and began pushing and shoving them off the Maidan . . . and the next day, when I went to visit Maidan, I didn't think I could go down empty-handed, given what everybody had been through. So as a sign, a gesture of peace, I brought sandwiches."[8]

The world media made so much of the wretched sandwiches that Nuland might have been better off distributing hand grenades. After the sandwiches saga, Russian secret services started monitoring Nuland's every move. On February 6, 2014, Russians leaked the transcript of a phone conversation between Nuland and Pyatt in which the two were matter-of-factly building a new government for Ukraine. It is not clear when exactly the conversation took place, but the State Department did not dispute its authenticity.

The three opposition leaders Nuland and Pyatt discussed, Arseniy Yatsenyuk, Oleh Tyahnybok, and Vitaliy Klichko, were Maidan favorites—Yatsenyuk a polished technocrat, Tyahnybok a crowd pleaser with a history of Jew bashing, Klichko a world champion heavyweight boxer. From the start, Pyatt and Nuland agreed they were all "in play." "Yats" (Yatsenyuk) would become prime minister. "Klitch" remained the "complicated electron" (Nuland: "I don't think Klitch should go into the government." Pyatt: "Just let him stay out and do his political homework and stuff"). The right-wing Tyahnybok "and his guys" were going to be a "problem." A deal had to be solidified soon, said Pyatt, because "the Russians will be working behind the scenes to try to torpedo it." Having by that time given up on the European Union's negotiating skills, Nuland now wanted to recruit the United Nations: "So that would be great, I think, to help glue this thing and to have the U.N. help glue it and, you know, fuck the E.U." "No, exactly," Pyatt agreed.[9]

Nuland's "Fuck the E.U." remark became notorious in Europe (a furious Angela Merkel called it "unacceptable"—the highest form of disapproval in diplomatic vernacular short of profanity), but the real harm was done in the east. Russians claimed they had caught Nuland and Pyatt red-handed at orchestrating regime change in Ukraine. Pyatt, interviewed by the press, refused to discuss "any phone calls" and claimed that his "role has been an appropriate diplomatic one": "I don't consider it meddling when we're in the business of helping to build bridges between the government and the opposition."[10]

Little wonder that with both Russia and America involved, the polarization of Ukraine sped up. But let's stop for a moment. We know that neoconservatives regard unseating a democratically elected president as permissible in a third-world country. But what was their plan for Ukraine, and what made them think they could achieve it (whatever it was) through the regime change?

Did they hope to promote Ukraine's association with the European Union? The reality was that no such association was possible without Russia's consent. Ukraine *and* Europe depended on Russian gas. If Putin chose to shut the tap—which he could do at any time—Europe would suffer, but Ukraine would fold.

Did they seek a closer partnership between Ukraine and NATO? It was no secret that the Ukrainian military remained in disheartening disarray. How could one possibly tease Ukraine's aggressive eastern neighbor by suggesting NATO expansion, when Ukraine did not stand a chance of deterring a preemptive assault, let alone defeating one? And what would NATO gain from such a conflict? Would most of the NATO powers even risk coming to Ukraine's defense? And what would happen to NATO's credibility—even the survival of the NATO treaty—if they did not?

Was the interventionists' goal "Westernization" of Ukrainian society? Leaving aside the unanswerable question about what exactly "Westernization" means, I would simply note that America had already tried introducing a "pro-Western" government in Ukraine in

2004, during the Orange Revolution, and that it did not work. Absent any effective system of checks and balances, the government remained corrupt, the economy stagnant. There was no reason to expect a revolution to succeed in 2014 where the earlier one had failed. In any case, any attempt at ousting Yanukovych, a lawfully elected president—even if an embezzler and a thug—was bound to anger eastern and southern Ukraine, his base of support. How would the United States benefit from a civil conflict in a nation of 44 million sitting on Russia's borders?

It does not seem as if American interventionists really had a plan for Ukraine. Most likely, their work in Kiev followed Napoleon's principle, famously appropriated by Lenin, *On s'engage, et puis on voit*—Let's engage, and take it from there.

After the Nuland-Pyatt leak, Europeans and Russians both stepped up their involvement in Kiev—Europeans offended, Russians enraged. Meanwhile, confrontations between government forces and protestors escalated. By February 20, at least seventy-seven people had died.

On February 21, Germany, France, Poland, and Russia brokered a compromise between the government and the Maidan. The opposition was represented by Nuland's and Pyatt's favorites: Yatsenyuk, Klichko, and Tyahnybok. Yanukovych signed for the government. Three E.U. foreign ministers signed as the agreement's guarantors: Radoslaw Sikorski of Poland, Frank-Walter Steinmeier of Germany, and Laurent Fabius of France. Called the "Agreement on the Settlement of Crisis in Ukraine," the document called for an "immediate end of bloodshed" and a "political resolution of the crisis." The signees pledged to form a national unity government. Presidential elections would be held "as soon as the new Constitution is adopted but no later than December 2014." "Recent acts of violence" would be investigated, the "authorities and the opposition will refrain from the use of violence," and the authorities "will not impose a state of emergency." The parliament would declare amnesty for "illegal actions" during the riots, and "illegal weapons should be handed over to the Ministry of Interior."[11]

The first international agreement to arise from the Ukrainian upheaval quickly became the first international document to collapse. Within hours after it was signed, Maidan rioters overtook government quarters. It is not clear who was behind the escalation, and it is not impossible that the resumed violence was spontaneous. What is clear is that opposition leaders used it to topple the regime, discarding any notion of "national unity."

Unable to take the stress anymore and apparently fearing for his life, Yanukovych left for eastern Ukraine—officially to attend a regional meeting of governors—and then disappeared. He would not resurface until February 28—in the Russian city of Rostov. Now leaderless, his faction in the parliament folded and voted with the opposition minority. The insurgency leaders declared the position of president vacant, formed an interim cabinet, scheduled presidential elections for May, and briefly banned the official use of the Russian language in Ukraine—a folly of grand magnitude.[12]

Putin: How to Respond?

What is often missed about Vladimir Putin's foreign policy is that it is largely reactive. Moscow deemed Western involvement in Ukraine unacceptable. If Ukraine forged a strong relationship with NATO, would that make the Russian Black Sea Fleet homeless *and* bring NATO troops to Sevastopol, the "City of Russian Glory"? After the United States' involvement in the Orange Revolution in 2004, every effort U.S. representatives made in Russia on behalf of the opposition was taken by the Kremlin as part of a conspiracy. The ease with which the United States now dropped a democratically elected president, Yanukovych, and gave unqualified recognition to insurgents in Kiev enraged the Kremlin. For the second time in ten years, America had supported, if not outright orches-trated, a regime change in Russia's "sister country." Was a coup in Moscow next?

NATO expansion and U.S. political engineering in the near abroad were two factors driving the strong Russian response to regime change in Kiev. The third was the domestic corrosion of Putin's regime.

In the winter of 2011–2012, Moscow saw a tide of spontane-ous grassroots protest. The authorities managed to overwhelm it bloodlessly, and Russian voters did put Putin in the Kremlin for a third term (officially, he got 63.6 percent of the vote, but even if the election was rigged, no poll or estimate puts his actual support below 55 percent). In Putin's "managed democracy," Russian living standards were possibly better than they had ever been (in 2013, 56 percent of Russians between the ages of eighteen and forty-five vacationed abroad). Yet the 2011–2012 protests signified the end of national accord. That had to be restored, and a "little victorious war" could do it.[13]

With President Yanukovych toppled and the interim cabinet sworn in, Kiev became ungovernable. Hundreds of Maidan riot-ers camped in government buildings and showed no intention of leaving. The ill-conceived ban on the official use of Russian lasted for just five days before being repealed, but in the meantime it had done a lot of damage. The Russophile media in Crimea, Donbass, and Odessa prophesied forced Ukrainization and pogroms coming from "fascists" in Kiev. Pro-Russian activists in eastern and south-ern Ukraine demanded secession and asked Russia for help. But Russia was not in a hurry.

The event that made Putin postpone any action was a pet proj-ect, the Winter Olympics in Sochi, scheduled for February 2014. Conceived as the triumphant symbol of Russia's resurrection from its years of chaos and poverty, carefully planned as a splendid display of national heritage and riches, and also extravagantly expensive, the Sochi Olympics were meant to be a coming-of-age fete for Putin's Russia. But the Western media did not take the hoped-for congratulatory tone. The correspondents' reports from Sochi were gleeful, sneering, and diminishing, suggesting an anti-Russian bias. As one American web site commented, "It got to the point where Western journalists in Sochi for Putin's overpriced Olympics were cheered like heroes for tweeting about how the curtains in their hotel rooms were falling down." A leading historian of Russia, Stephen F. Cohen, called the coverage "toxic."[14]

As Putin and the Russian street saw it, no matter what Russia tried, in the eyes of the West it was never good enough. The president sat calmly through the Winter Games.

PART II

Peninsula of Sun and War

FOUR

History

The "little green men," or "polite soldiers," as local Russophiles affectionately called them, first appeared on Crimean streets in the last week of February 2014. Masked and silent, they wore green camouflage uniforms without any insignia and would not reveal their identity; they had clearly come from elsewhere, were very knowledgeable concerning the whereabouts of Ukrainian troops, and were armed with Russian military weapons. Sometimes mixing with the grassroots Russian militias, sometimes leading them, often pretending to *be* them, the strangers took over government buildings, train stations, and airports, and blocked Ukrainian forces in their bases. Surrounded by these armed men, the Crimean parliament appointed a new government, which in turn quickly scheduled a referendum on whether Crimea should secede from Ukraine and join Russia.

Ostensibly to protect the ethnic Russian population in Crimea and potentially elsewhere, Putin asked the Russian parliament to authorize the use of troops in Ukraine. On March 1, the parliament obliged. By then, in reality, the stealth invasion was well under way, and the "little green men" were already on the ground in Crimea.

Russia's annexation of Crimea was a reactive act, a hard-power response to American involvement in the Kiev crisis, which had culminated in a regime change. It is difficult to dispute that Russia had legitimate strategic interests on the Crimean Peninsula. Sevastopol was the Russian Black Sea Fleet's only major base, and the revolutionary Euromaidan had made the Kremlin believe it might be slipping away. No American leader had seriously considered adding Ukraine to NATO, but several who were no longer in a position to make anything of the kind happen, including former secretary of state Hillary Clinton, pretended that it had to be done. The noise such statements made hid their hollowness from the Russian ear. By striking in Crimea, Moscow believed it was preemptively getting control over the peninsula before NATO arrived.

Not some piecemeal or creeping expansion, but a brazen gambit, the annexation announced to the world that Russia had "risen from her knees" (in Putin's words), that the country was strong and determined to defend its spheres of influence, by military force, if necessary. After years of warning the West that interfering in Ukraine would be crossing the red line, the Kremlin felt it could not but respond.

No other aggression could be sold to the Russian public so easily. Most Russians could be expected to support the action because Crimea was a national fetish that had ended up in Ukraine accidentally, due to a bit of political pandering by Nikita Khrushchev in 1954.

"Revolutions" of Crimea

The term "revolutions of Crimea," meaning cycles of violent transfer of power from one dominant group to another, comes from eighteenth- and nineteenth-century European visitors. They used the term "revolution" as in "revolving door," not as in "overthrow of a government in favor of a new order." Such cycles seem to be the structural framework of Crimea's history.

Crimea is a natural lure; a fat piece of low-hanging fruit dangling from the continent's underbelly, strikingly warmer and lusher than the adjoining northern plains. The eighteenth-century British traveler Elizabeth Craven compared its steppes to "the finest green velvet"; the Tatar nickname for Crimea is Yesil Ada, or Green Isle.[1]

It sits on a busy intersection. In the past, peoples that had never heard of it—early nomadic groups like the Huns, Goths, and Kipchaks—still found themselves at its doors while traversing the east-to-west corridor across Eurasia.

Crimea is also a trap. It is very close to being an island, and like an island, it is difficult to evacuate in case of a foreign invasion. The Perekop Isthmus, just four miles wide, is too narrow to let one dodge an invading army, and the Kerch Strait, two miles across, is uncomfortably wide to traverse by boat. As hard as it is to leave physically, it is almost as hard to let go emotionally. Every group exiled or pushed out from Crimea has mourned the loss of Eden ever since, perpetuating the separation trauma for future generations. There has never been a unique Crimean product or resource that would be a hot commodity on world markets, except for the peninsula itself, a fetish in many cultures, epitomizing comfortable living in an accommodating environment.

For the people of the north—first nomads, then Slavs—Crimea was the most verdant place they had ever seen. For the people of the Mediterranean—Greeks, Jews, Italians—it was the northernmost breath of familiar terrain. Significantly colder than Attica, Liguria, or Palestine, it was nevertheless recognizable, acceptable, homelike.

For a place the size of Massachusetts—ten thousand square miles —Crimea is extraordinarily diverse: steppes, salt marshes, a desert, three mountain ranges, five plateaus, a subtropical littoral. Until the mid–twentieth century, its population was comparably diverse: Tatar, Turk, Russian, Ukrainian, German, Karaite, Jewish, Armenian, Bulgarian, Italian, Greek. With only a certain degree of exaggeration, a medieval visitor from Europe reported that nearly every settlement along the South Shore had its own language.[2]

Crimea's history is of successive waves of colonization: early nomads; Greeks and Romans; Byzantines; Genoese and Venetians; Tatars and Ottoman Turks; Russians and Ukrainians. Alongside the dominant groups came minorities. Never noticeable politically, Armenians, Jews, Germans, and others were yeast to the peninsula's economy. Maintaining close ties with their kin overseas, *they* had shaped Crimea's cosmopolitan character and made it a hub of maritime trade. Though locked together in a small space, these ethnicities and their economies did not merge. Crimea developed not as a melting pot but as a salad bowl. Each of its urban neighborhoods had a distinct ethnic character, as did the villages in the countryside.

On a macro level, Crimea falls into three distinct zones: the steppes, the mountains, and the littoral. "Its northeastern division is a steppe and has neither tree nor hill, but its southern part presents a far different appearance, the mountains rising to a considerable height and encircling valleys of great beauty and fertility," an early U.S. Navy manual says. To an American eye, the gently rolling Crimean steppes resemble the Great Plains—and the South Shore, the Pacific coast.[3]

In the days of horseback travel, the steppe took five days to cross north to south. Traditionally, it belonged to nomads—Taurii, Cimmerians, Scythians, Sarmatians, Goths, Huns, Kipchaks. The historian Brian G. Williams writes: "From the dawn of recorded history, the plains of the northern Black Sea were dominated by nomads who mounted hardy steppe ponies, mastered the deadly art of mounted archery and fought one another for control over the rich pasture lands." The weapons and strategy applied in this endless struggle remained basic yet effective. According to estimates by Edward N. Luttwak, a nomadic expeditionary force could cover between thirty and fifty miles per day "for quite a few days in a row." The army of the strongest sedentary state in the region, Byzantium, could not exceed fifteen.[4]

According to Brian G. Williams's history of the region, the "losers in these largely unrecorded struggles" for control of the steppes "were either absorbed by the victors or scattered into mountain ranges of the south": the Crimean mountains served as "a sanctuary for tribes and ethnic groups fleeing the waves of more powerful nomadic groups." One group, the Goths, maintained a steady presence in the mountains for centuries. The commercial nations of the Mediterranean occupied the littoral.[5]

The steppe, the mountains, and the littoral tended to have amazingly little contact with each other—three separate realms on the meager ten thousand square miles, meeting mostly at border trading posts. Ruins of miniature but sturdy fortifications still block every north-to-south gorge connecting the littoral to the plateau. Built fifteen centuries ago by the order of a Byzantine emperor, and differently referred to by later visitors as "castles," "fortresses," or just "walls," in their prime they sealed every hole in the mountain range. A small Byzantine garrison guarded each one, wardens of a rich realm threatened by marauders. Most of them stood in clear visibility of each other, meaning that every suspicious activity on the border, let alone a breach, would be swiftly communicated along the whole security perimeter.[6]

Until the first time the Russians conquered Crimea, in 1783, the littoral region existed independently from the rest of the peninsula. Greeks developed it in the seventh century BCE; Romans and Byzantines maintained what the Greeks had left them; and so later did the merchant republics of Genoa and Venice. No Mediterranean power ever tried annexing the rest of the peninsula. The only thing

Mediterraneans wanted in Crimea was a string of trading posts, and the littoral, the meeting place of the Asiatic steppe and the Mediterranean city, served the purpose. The littoral received little investment, and no significant public buildings or urban spreads. What the maritime people needed was port facilities, fortresses, and a handful of northbound highways.

Europeans used Crimea as a mudroom, Europe's easternmost port of entry, a place were you dress up for the journey or unwind on completing one. Constantinople was just two days away by sail—by Middle Ages standards, practically a commuting distance. For Silk Road businessmen like Marco Polo, it was the last respite before stepping into the unknown, the edge of the familiar world. It did not merit more than two lines in Polo's book of travels ("taking their departure from Constantinople," the merchants reach a "port named Soldaia," whence the longest leg of their eastward journey started). These settlements became the foundation for Crimea's future urban structure. The majority of Crimean cities and towns—Sevastopol, Yevpatoria, Feodosia, Kerch, Alushta—grew on antiquity's humus.[7]

The only formidable structures Mediterraneans ever built on the peninsula, fortresses, came into disuse long ago and now exist mostly as ruins. To see majesty beyond neglect and decay, one has to refer to their Italian prototypes in Liguria and Golfo della Spezza (the Genoese castle in Crimean Gurzuf, for example, was modeled on the fortress in Lerice). For the Republic of Genoa, the Crimean littoral and its eastward continuation on the Sea of Azov were important enough to deserve a special bureau in the central government, the Office of Gazaria (as Italians called the area at the time).

In addition to the Silk Road, filling Crimean warehouses with spices, pearls, cloth, and precious stones, the coast served the northbound route to what later would become Ukraine and Russia. From the river Don came a novelty—caviar, the salted fish eggs of sturgeon. Slavic merchants brought furs and slaves. Even Catholic missionaries did not have to think twice before buying a boy when in need of a companion for a long journey to heathens' lands. Because Italians preferred light-skin people, Russian, Polish, and Ukrainian slaves were in greatest demand.[8]

Everything could be sold and bought in Kaffa, the main port and trading center for the Genoese, and now known as Feodosia. Horrified by the sight of "fathers selling their children and brother selling brother," tavern owners offering lodgers "young virgins for a measure of wine," a Spanish traveler called the city the place of evil doings, theft, and wickedness.[9]

The three Crimean realms—the steppe, the mountains, and the littoral—hang in a fragile balance, overlapping only tentatively. That changed when a new nomadic group invaded from the north: Mongols.

Clash of Civilizations

The Turkic name for the peninsula is Kirim—"fortress." Other languages adopted this term; the English "Crimea," or Russian and Ukrainian "Krym," all originate in corrupted Turkic.

As the inhabitants of Crimea were ignorant of the scope, charge, and potential of the Mongol conquests, their invasion at first looked like any other. But the Mongols were the first group in history to occupy the whole of the peninsula, not just the steppe but the mountains and littoral too.

The Genoese colonies proved difficult to subdue. War for the littoral lasted for several decades. A freak yet monumental consequence was the Black Death pandemic in Europe. Plague bacterium lives on the arid plains of Central Asia, and advancing west, the Mongols had to cross those. The Mongol army group that besieged Genoese Kaffa in 1346 suffered an outbreak of the disease causing more casualties than war. Their commanders ordered the Mongols to catapult the dead bodies into the besieged city—perhaps the earliest occasion when biological warfare was employed. The Genoese colonists fleeing Kaffa carried the disease to Constantinople and then to Italy, thus triggering the catastrophe that eventually killed at least 75 million people.[10]

Within two generations after their invasion of Crimea, the Mongols adopted Islam. Genghis Khan and his generation had worshiped "Tengri, the god of the blue sky," but in the early 1300s a ruler of the Golden Horde together with his aristocracy converted to Sunni Islam. Crimea saw its first mosque built in 1314.[11]

The peninsula became part of *umma*, the global Muslim community, and of the Dar al-Islam, or House of Islam, metaphysically opposed to the lands of unbelievers, Dar al-Harb, the House of War. Meanwhile, across the sea in the Balkans and Anatolia, a new hegemonic power emerged: the Ottoman Empire. With the Golden Horde's conversion, Mongols and Turks now shared a cultural space.[12]

The Ottomans' clash with the Byzantines and the West transcended the standard pattern of struggling for territory and resources. What had started as a border war grew into a clash of three civilizations—Islamic, Eastern Orthodox, and Western.

For a century, Crimea remained a province of the Golden Horde; as the Mongol empire weakened, it broke away to form the Crimean Khanate. This was ruled by a Genghizid, as Mongol custom dictated, but its independence was short-lived (1443–1475). War flared up between clans, pretenders, the Italians, and the still unconquered mountaineer Goths. After a faction of clan leaders asked the Ottomans for help, the Ottomans landed in Crimea, defeated every party, and turned the peninsula into their protectorate.

The Ottoman era in Crimean history did not cancel the structures laid down before but built upon them. The Ottomans let the khanate control the steppes and the mountains, but they claimed the littoral as their own, turning it into a province of the empire. Unlike previous Mediterranean colonizers, they took over the whole coastal perimeter and built fortresses along its entire length, the biggest at the northern gateways, Perekop and Arabat, and then continued the line of coastal fortifications east and west. The Black Sea became known as the Ottoman Lake.[13]

The Ottoman Empire's government, known as the Sublime Porte, is largely absent from the twenty-first-century Western conversation about Crimea, Russia, and Ukraine, and this is unfortunate because its impact on the area was no less significant and lasting than Kiev's or Moscow's. Not content with mere conquest of the Black Sea steppe, the Ottomans aspired to be a transforming economic force in the area. Imperial overstretch forced the abandonment of the most daring (and expensive) projects, but in the mid–sixteenth century the empire attempted to build a canal connecting the Don and Volga rivers—and thus two seas, the Black and the Caspian—a bold engineering venture that was not accomplished until four centuries later, by the Soviet Union, and was deemed so amazing even in 1951 that Stalin asked Sergei Prokofiev to write a celebratory symphony for the occasion.[14]

The Ottomans deftly developed the urban structure and trade routes they had inherited. Kaffa became the coastal Ottoman capital, and grew into a thriving trade hub, routinely referred to as Kuchuk Stamboul—Little Istanbul. With a population ranging between 70,000 and 100,000, Kaffa ranked as the eighth-largest city in the Ottoman Empire, after Istanbul, Cairo, Aleppo, Damascus, Bursa, Adrianople, and Salonika. As practiced in other parts of the empire, in Kaffa the Ottomans tolerated the presence of other ethnic groups as long as they remained economically useful—Jews, Italians, Greeks, and the largest minority, Armenians, reportedly maintaining more than twenty churches in the city.[15]

The capital of the khanate, Bakhchisaray, was by comparison a sad little affair. The entrance to the palace of the khans carried the Genghizid dynastic symbol, the *tamgha* trident, but the khanate could not live up to the dynasty's legacy. The only port the khanate was allowed to keep was the smallish Goezleve (Yevpatoria) on the underdeveloped western coast, its sole adornment the graceful Juma Jami Mosque, designed by the Ottoman architect of genius Mimar Sinan at the peak of the khanate's might. A miniature variation on the Suleymaniye Mosque in Istanbul and modest compared with Sinan's great works, the Juma Jami still supplied the city with a distinguished silhouette, its dome identifiable fifteen miles off.[16]

In the twentieth century, when Crimean Tatar intellectuals were reinventing their nation, the khanate's statehood became a principal issue. Having a fully independent state in one's past was viewed as indispensable to a national creation myth. This resulted in a lively revisionist discourse that gave rise to widely divergent descriptions of the relationship between Bakhchisaray and Istanbul. According to most historians, the Giray dynasty that ruled the Crimean Khanate "recognized Ottoman suzerainty" and served as Istanbul's "vassals"; but in the nationalists' view, the "two states existed in a tense, respectful alliance," the Giray khans "more allies than subjects," and the khanate had "partial independence" while enjoying the "protection of the Ottoman sultans, who regarded it as a valuable bulwark against the Russians."[17]

In the language of modern political science, the khanate most closely fits the definition of a "client state." On one hand, Bakhchisaray minted its own coins and maintained diplomatic relations with Russia and Poland. On the other, each Genghizid claiming succession rights traveled to Istanbul to be approved and anointed by the Ottoman sultan, the Sunni Caliph. When required by Istanbul, Crimean cavalry fought for the sultan throughout the region, making a critical contribution in many battles, including the sieges of Vienna in 1529 and 1683. The Ottoman coastal fortresses, originally meant to keep an eye on the Tatars, also guarded Crimea from the occasional Russo-Ukrainian amphibious raids.[18]

The Tatar core of the khanate consisted of three groups: Nogai (Kipchak) nomads, Tat mountaineers, and Yaliboyu coastal dwellers. An eighteenth-century British visitor, Maria Guthrie, described three different "races of men" on the peninsula. The Nogai were "distinguished by high cheek bones" and looked exactly like the "Huns of ancient authors, who committed such horrible ravages in Europe in old times." The Tat had "round, and rather ruddy faces, and stout well-made bodies," while the Yaliboyu were "distinguished by a dark complexion and a rather longish face, with features much more resembling the European" than the "frightful" Huns.[19]

In Turkic languages, "Tat" refers to conquered people, and in the hierarchy of the khanate Tats sat the lowest, with a special cabinet minister of the khan, "Lord of the Tats," regulating their affairs.[20] The Yaliboyu on the littoral were understandably the closest to the Ottomans, and their upper classes had absorbed the culture of Turkish Anatolia. The most numerous group, the nomadic Nogai in the north, made up the bulk of the khanate's army, and the incessant raids plaguing Ukraine, Russia, and Poland were more Nogai than "Tatar."[21]

The economy of the khanate was based on pillaging and the slave trade. As the raids pursued material benefit more than anything else, they were executed not only by the khan's army but also by troops loyal to individual aristocrats (*beys*). In addition to sustaining the state bursary and the aristocracy, they also served to weaken and destroy Slavic settlements on the steppes. One of the most famous campaigns was Khan Devlet Giray's attack on Moscow in May 1571, when his troops burned down everything in the Russian capital except for the Kremlin walls, which were made of brick. The Russian tsar at the time was none other than Ivan the

Terrible. Remembered as a successful empire builder, he was pow-
erless against the khanate's cavalry.[22]

Kaffa became the largest center of slave trading in Eastern Europe. A Polish historian estimates that Poland lost a million people
to Tatar raiders between 1550 and 1694. A Soviet historian argued
that eastern Ukraine lost a hundred thousand a year.[23]

The peninsula's agriculture was supported in the mountain valleys by Tats. Finance, trade, and crafts were in the hands of Greeks,
Armenians, and Karaites living mostly on the Ottoman littoral.[24]

The war between Russia and Crimea, which went on for four centuries, had nothing to do with grand strategy. The Ottoman Empire
was already overstretched and could not possibly have been interested in subjugating Russia or wresting Ukraine away from Poland.
The goal of the Ottomans and their Crimean client state was to
maintain Russia and Ukraine as a permanent source of slaves.

At first, Russia's military goal was just basic security in the south.
Until the 1600s, the Crimean Khanate remained the stronger
power, but even after the two had reached military equilibrium, the
annual devastation of its southern provinces depleted Russia's labor
pool and kept the local economy at a subsistence level. As the Russian state strengthened, it found another goal in the war against the
Crimean Khanate: to annex the fertile black earth belt, the Wild
Fields, where Nogai Tatars lived. Later, still another motivation
emerged: Russia's perceived place in the clash of civilizations.

The Third Rome

In an essay written in 1985 called "Flight from Byzantium," a med-
itative Istanbul travelogue, Joseph Brodsky talks about observing
"the aircraft carriers of the Third Rome sailing slowly through the
gates of the Second on their way to the First."[25] The trope is more
meaningful than elegant.

The "Third Rome" concept is a noxious perennial of Russian history. Formulated around 1511 by an ecclesiastic named Philotheus from the Pskov Eleazer Monastery, it announced that after the fall of Rome and then of the Second Rome (Constantinople) because of their transgressions against true Christianity, the center of the world had moved to Moscow. "Two Romes have fallen, a third stands, a fourth there shall not be." Within a few decades, this grand concept grew into Russian state doctrine. Not only did the princes of Moscow reinvent themselves as "tsars," a corruption of "Caesar." As James H. Billington puts it in his seminal interpretation of Russian history *The Icon and the Axe*, "All of Muscovy came to be viewed as a kind of vast monastery under the discipline of a Tsar-Archimandrite."[26]

An upstart community stuck on the periphery of Christianity *and* Islam, destitute even by the forgiving standards of sixteenth-century Europe, suddenly imagined itself the leader of humankind. Here is what made this happen.

After the fall of Constantinople in 1453, Russia became the only Orthodox country still standing. Its place in world affairs remained utterly humble—precisely the reason it had been allowed to survive, as no foreign conqueror was interested in the cold and wet patch of landlocked woods that was Russia at the time. It is not even mentioned in *The Alexiad*, a war and diplomacy treatise by the twelfth-century Byzantine princess Anna Komnene.[27] To reformulate their country, Russians needed an intellectual push from the outside; it appears to have come from an exceptional European woman, Princess Sophia Palaeolog. Born Zoe, the niece of the last Byzantine emperor, and raised as a ward of Pope Paul II, she was married off to the grand prince of Moscow, Ivan III, in 1472. One example of her strong influence on her husband and his court is the Kremlin: the architects invited to build it came from Italy, and its walls and towers bear a striking resemblance to the Milan castle of the Sforzas, from the color of the bricks to the swallowtail merlons.

Sophia believed Russia could ally with Catholic Europe against the Ottomans and reclaim her ancestral Constantinople for her children. The concept of Rome as a wandering imperial capital had been the foundation of Constantinople (Anna Komnene mentions in passing that "power was transferred from Rome to our country and the Queen of Cities"). Though centered in the east, the empire still called itself "Roman"; the misleading term "Byzantium" did not come into general use in European languages until the nineteenth century.[28]

The Third Rome was part of Sophia's dowry, and came from the Byzantine ecclesiastical tradition, yet Moscow had little sway in the Greek-speaking parts of Christendom. However, all Slavic Orthodox territories, such as Serbia, Bulgaria, and of course Ukraine, shared a sacred language with Russians—the Church Slavonic, adapted from the ninth-century Macedonian dialect. That made the Third Rome transnational community possible—"imaginable," in Benedict Anderson's words. To use another term from Anderson, the Third Rome concept was nothing but "territorialization of faith."[29]

In later centuries, the idea became Russia's damnation. Peter the Great, an adept of realpolitik, saw little value in waging war against the Ottomans when a shorter way to Europe lay in the north. But for later Romanovs, "returning the cross" to the top of the Hagia Sophia in Constantinople became an obligation. Pursuing the mirage of the Third Rome, they dragged Russia into one war after another in the Black Sea area and in the Balkans. As late as World War I, to keep Russia as an ally, Britain and France promised Tsar Nicholas II Constantinople, the Bosporus, the Sea of Marmara, and the Dardanelles. After World War II, Stalin demanded that Turkey hand over control of the straits (the Bosporus and the Dardanelles), a push that made the White House respond with the Truman Doctrine, explicitly protecting Turkey and Greece from Russian aggression.

For Russians, the road to Constantinople started in Crimea. Russian troops stormed Perekop in 1736 and sacked most of the peninsula before being forced to withdraw. The next generation of generals was more successful. In 1771, Russians again occupied the peninsula; this time, the Ottoman government in Kaffa evacuated to Istanbul.

Russia's ruler at the time was Catherine the Great. Far ahead of her time, extraordinarily successful in her conquests and diplomacy, she and her inner circle of advisers made the grandiose decision that Crimea would be a stepping-stone in the transformation of the eastern Mediterranean. Catherine was certain that the Ottoman Empire was ready to crumble. Having named her eldest grandson after Alexander the Great, she named the second Constantine, as he was destined to be the king of Constantinople, the capital of a "Greek monarchy." Her lover, Grigory Potemkin, would become king of "Dacia"—an imagined country roughly contiguous with modern Romania. She modestly referred to this entire plan as her "Greek Project."[30]

Catherine's conquests on the Black Sea met with widespread approval in Europe. The Ottoman Empire was a traditional foe that had last laid siege to Vienna just a century earlier. Feeling very secure, Catherine started with an experiment: in 1774, Russia and Turkey signed a treaty establishing Crimea as an independent state. For the Ottomans, the khanate would be a buffer zone, and for Catherine a test site for what would centuries later be called "nation-building." Her Greek monarchy and Dacia would have to be built from the Ottoman bureaucratic and social fabric. She thought Crimea was perfect for trying this out.

Khan Shagin Giray, whom she supported in Bakhchisaray, saw himself as a Crimean Peter the Great—a modernizer who would borrow technology and governmental structures from Europe. Catherine returned the littoral to the khanate and took care of its bursary. As an attempt at social engineering, Catherine's Crimean project anticipated later Western efforts in the non-Western world. While its stated good intentions, such as social reform and modernization, are impossible to prove or disprove, the pragmatism of the strategy is as valid now as it was in Catherine's day: to raise a junior ally whose new (Westernized) elites would be completely dependent on the creator.[31]

And not unlike the twenty-first-century attempts at nation-building, Catherine's Crimea project collapsed. The experiment had a bloody ending—civil war—unsurprisingly so because the khan was rightly seen as a puppet of an alien power. In 1783, Russia squashed the rebellion and annexed Crimea.

Catherine dismissed the failed experiment in Crimea as a freak loss, still sure that the Greek monarchy and Dacia would succeed. To demonstrate her commitment to the development of the conquered Ottoman lands and to celebrate her victory in the clash of civilizations, in 1787 she put herself through the terrible inconvenience of visiting Crimea in person, with European ambassadors and the emperor of Austria in tow.

The six-month journey proved monumental, belonging among the top PR campaigns in history. Catherine was delighted by what she saw and proclaimed Crimea the "Garden of Eden." Having failed to engineer change on the peninsula through its government, she now launched a massive campaign of colonization.[32]

Catherine reimagined Crimea as a Russian Greece to exist alongside Moscow, the Third Rome. The territories of the khanate were divided into three provinces: Kherson and Yekaterinoslav on the mainland steppe, and Taurida as the Crimean peninsula per se. The name Taurida reflected Catherine's Greek pretensions for the place, as did the names of two major cities she started on the peninsula—Sevastopol and Simferopol. Kaffa and Goezleve had their ancient Greek names restored: Feodosia and Yevpatoria, respectively.

Tellingly, the rest of the toponyms were kept Turkic, with *su* for "river," *dahg* for "mountain," and *gol* for "lake." Catherine ruled by corruption, not coercion. Tatar nobles were given Russian nobility, land grants, and power over the previously free peasantry. With the aristocracy thus brought over to her side, revolts on the peninsula remained few and insignificant. Catherine also brought in new settlers: the steppes had hardly any tradition of agriculture.

Although international trade was considerable (the port of Yevpatoria alone received 170 foreign ships a year), the peninsula's export-import structure did not look satisfactory. Crimea exported salt from the Perekop marshes, wool, and sheepskin—both products of semi-nomadic Tatar shepherds. From the Mediterranean, it imported silk and cotton cloth, wine, lemons, oranges, chestnuts, olives, apples, dates, coffee, and tobacco. From mainland Russia, wheat, butter, and linen came, and also one telling item, locks, exceeding eighteen thousand a year—clear evidence of the redistribution of property. Importing items like oranges and coffee was unavoidable, but the Garden of Eden was certainly capable of producing more domestically. The list the colonizers came up with included wheat, wine, silk, raisins, almonds, figs, prunes, olives, capers, herring, anchovies, and oysters. Having little regard for Russian and Ukrainian peasantry, the empress invited farmers from abroad, starting with her home country, Germany.[33]

Within two decades, Crimea's South Shore became popular with the imperial aristocracy. Some built summer retreats, others moved to the littoral permanently—a quaint community consisting of devoted agriculturalists excited by the opportunities the subtropical climate offered, retirees disenchanted with the metropolitan glamour, spiritualists seeking seclusion, and former courtiers marred by scandal.[34]

Mary Holderness, an intrepid British traveler who spent four years in the village of Karagoz in eastern Crimea between 1816 and 1820, left a detailed account of her sojourn on the peninsula. I am unable to find a good explanation for why a British woman would move to a very basic settlement in the wooded hills, easily a day's journey from the nearest town. But others did the same thing; something about Crimea appealed to restive spirits, the kind of people who in later centuries would move to Tangier or Bali.

Mary Holderness caught Crimean diversity at its peak: all the people of the khanate were still there, and the government's resettlement campaign had added newcomers. In the towns of Crimea, Holderness reported, one could find the "descendants of more than fifteen different nations."[35] Like most travelers, Holderness had carried her prejudices with her and brought them back home unchanged; the classification of Crimeans she suggests tells us at least as much about a colonizer's mindset as about the people she was observing.

She found the "habits and modes of agriculture" of the Tatars "rude and simple," their wealth still consisting "in flocks and herds." The Nogai Tatars, she thought, had fared especially poorly, despite the Russian government's efforts to conquer the "inveterate prejudices of this wandering horde" and induce them to take up farming. "They are, however, of all the colonists, far the worst cultivators; and are still much addicted to grazing large flocks and herds, and numerous studs of mares."[36]

According to Holderness, the largest minorities were Greeks and Germans, each constituting about 10 percent of the population. "The occupations of the Greeks are perhaps more various than those of most of the settlers. In the towns they are found as respectable merchants, as small shopkeepers. . . . The Greeks also are the only fishers who adventure far for the purpose of fishing."[37]

The German Mennonites, or Moravians, in the steppes "came over with plenty of money, knowledge of business, and superior industry, and are at present a wealthy race; having built large farmhouses and offices, planted extensive orchards, and laid out great gardens, possessing the finest breed of cows in the country, and growing a great abundance of corn." But a different group of Germans, the Swabians, she found low and brutal in their manners, "the least civilized inhabitants of the Crimea."[38]

"The Bulgarians, though ranking low in point of numbers amongst the other colonists of New Russia, are perhaps deserving the first notice, from the high character they bear, as a sober, industrious, and meritorious class. . . . As agriculturalists, the Bulgarians hold also pre-eminence amongst their neighbours."

The Armenians were "universally resident in the towns, either as merchants or burghers; and the application so contemptuously bestowed by Buonaparte on the English, seems, in truth, perfectly applicable to these people—they are really a nation of shopkeepers."[39]

"The Jews are very numerous indeed in all the colonies, composing from one-fifth to one-tenth of the whole population. But they are, with very few exceptions, fixed in the class of burghers and shopkeepers, in every one of the towns of New Russia." The Karaites, a Jewish group speaking a Turkic language and not recognizing rabbinical authority or the Talmud, were "commonly the most wealthy, and are on all accounts the most respectable. They hold themselves very distinct from their Polish brethren." They "aver that they were no way concerned in, or consenting to," Jesus Christ's death, and "thus reject the dreadful responsibility entailed on them by the declaration of their forefathers—'His blood be on us, and on our children.'"[40]

A few French and Swiss; some Poles ("tall, and finely formed: even the servants are superior in their manners to any other of the peasantry"). "The gypsies of the Crimea, called Tsigans, resemble in habits and appearance those of England, and, like them, exist chiefly by plunder. They are commonly the musicians at weddings, profess fortune-telling, and have all the tricks and cant of begging."[41]

Among the minorities Holderness described, three groups had been on the peninsula before the Russian conquest and even before the Tatars: Greeks, Armenians, and Karaites. Their salad bowl coexistence encouraged a niche economy: Armenians controlled exports of salt, with a town in the salt-producing area bearing the name Armenian Bazar; a thriving community of Karaites in Yevpatoria carried on commerce with Constantinople and the Levant.[42]

Theoretically, in Crimea, Catherine practiced something we might call laissez-faire multiculturalism, yet in the process, the Tatar community got severely undermined. The Russians prided themselves on letting Crimean Muslims practice their faith, but at the same time, with the arrogance typical of a "civilizing" nation, they forced the Nogai Tatars to take up agriculture, eradicating the nomadic economy of the steppes and damaging the old social fabric.

The Crimean Tatar concept of land and property was based on the interpretation of *shariat*, or Islamic law, and the nomadic tradition. No one could claim ownership over forests, steppes, wells, and pastures belonging to the whole umma. Twenty-five percent of Crimean lands were *vakif*—endowments donated to religious institutions. After a short period of accommodation, the Russian government started confiscating the vakif lands. A mass exodus of Tatars began. By the end of the eighteenth century, around 120,000 out of the population of 300,000 had left for the Ottoman Empire. In mystical terms, this was a *hijra*, religious repatriation from the land of unbelievers to the Dar al-Islam. That left their economic niches and property up for grabs, enticing more settlers to come: Bulgarians, Greeks, and Armenians from the Ottoman Empire, and Rabbinite Jews from Poland.[43]

The Romanov who revived Catherine's Greek Project was her grandson, Nicholas I. His push onto Ottoman lands culminated in the invasion of the two Danube principalities—Moldavia and

Wallachia—in 1853. For Nicholas, this was a crusade, an effort to retake Muslim-controlled lands and restore them to Christian rule. But the days when the Russian victories over the sultan's armies were trumpeted in Europe as a triumph of "Christianity" against "Islam" were gone. Russo-European solidarity had been short-lived and opportunistic. The great powers of Europe had stopped viewing Turkey as a threat to their interests and were now worried about a new challenger—none other than Nicholas's empire. The leading Western power at the time, Britain, found itself confronted by a Russian onslaught on two fronts—in the Balkans and Central Asia. The latter clash had come to be known as the Great Game. It was not an actual war, as it was not feasible strategically to fight a meaningful campaign on the fringes of Afghanistan and Tibet. The Black Sea was a different matter. Responding to the Russian invasion, a British-French force landed in Crimea with support from the Ottomans and the Italian kingdom of Piedmont. The goal was to intimidate Russia enough to ensure Turkey's continued existence.[44]

The Crimean War of 1853–1856 turned out to be a seminal conflict in the history of nineteenth-century Europe. For the first time, Russia found Europe united in its determination to check Russian expansion. This pattern, a European coalition facing a lone Russian aggressor, would often recur.

Geopolitically, the British-French strategy was brilliantly asymmetrical: "You assail our interests on the periphery, we punch you in the gut." To demonstrate their advantage over Russia's purely land-based power, Britain and France also sent fleets to attack Kamchatka in the Pacific and Archangel on the White Sea, and made a showy appearance at the doorstep of St. Petersburg, the imperial capital on the Baltic Sea (the Romanovs grimly watched from shore).

Initially landing in Kalamita Bay north of Sevastopol, the Allied force took hold of the western part of the Crimean peninsula. The fighting almost immediately focused on Sevastopol, where the siege of the city lasted for 349 days.[45]

The war ended in a crushing defeat for Russia, but not before 450,000 Russian servicemen, 100,000 French, and 20,000 British died. The subsequent peace treaty required Russia to stay away from Ottoman territories and barred it from having a navy in the Black Sea, but the humiliation prompted the period known in Russian history as the Great Reforms—including emancipation of the serfs and the introduction of a jury system in the courts, to name just two. Russia recuperated fast, and despite the treaty resumed its attacks on the Ottomans in the Balkans. Independent Bulgaria, Montenegro, Romania, and Serbia were products of these campaigns. The most lasting impacts of the Crimean War were cultural: it was the first war in history to receive daily coverage in the press. Just as Florence Nightingale and "The Charge of the Light Brigade" became canonical pieces of British patriotic myth, the tragic perseverance of Russian troops in Crimea, particularly in Sevastopol, entered the Russian national pantheon. One writer laid down the foundations of this mythology: the young artillery officer Leo Tolstoy, in *The Sebastopol Sketches*.[46]

Another lasting effect of the war happened in Crimea. Accused of collaborating with the invading allies, Tatars once again departed for Turkey in large numbers. Aside from the fact that the colonizer was not entitled to any loyalty of the colonized, the Tatars had a language, culture, and religion in common with the Turkish troops. In any case, the anti-Russian hostilities were largely limited to the pillaging of Russian landlords' estates.[47]

This second exodus started in 1860 and 1861. Some 135,000 Tatars left, roughly 40 percent of the Crimean Tatar community. It does not seem that Russian reprisals against the Tatars were gross or consistent enough to cause the flight. Scholars suggest that the general feeling of insecurity made the community "prone to calls for migration" from religious leaders. In other words, social distress manifested itself in religious terms. Tatars leaving for the Ottoman Empire identified as *muhajir,* Muslims fleeing a homeland occupied by unbelievers to reunite with the Dar al-Islam.[48]

For Russian and Ukrainian farmers, the departures were an opportunity. Tens of thousands of Slavs moved into the areas vacated by the Tatars. That should not have been a cause for celebration: Crimea may be fertile, but the chronic lack of water makes it a precarious garden. Experience, knowledge, and skills had departed with the Tatars. One example would be camels: widely and wisely used by Tatars in the arid parts of the peninsula, they were branded "Asiatic" and "backward" by settlers, to be quickly replaced by horses, which were not always suitable for the terrain. "No settler, Russian, Bulgarian, or German, would ever be able to create gardens and vineyards" that perfect "on a terrain foreign to him," Princess Yelena Gorchakova sighed. Another Russian visitor wrote: "Every person who has spent at least a month in Crimea knows that with the Tatar exodus Crimea died." Huge areas in the steppes began looking like "the coasts of the Dead Sea," and the whole of Crimea was like a "house after a fire." The second Tatar exodus sealed the fate of the peninsula. From then on, the Kirim people would always be a minority in the land of their ancestors.[49]

With Tatars leaving and new settlers coming, Crimea was developing as a confusing cultural mosaic, with old landmarks receding or gone, and new ones in the making. In Russian discourse, the empire had defeated "Oriental" backwardness in Crimea through "Occidental" modernization. Crimean towns came to be divided into what was called "new," or "European," and "Asiatic," or "Tatar," parts. The European neighborhoods faced the sea; the Tatar opening up on the steppes or the mountains. "Nothing of particular interest" could be found in the "Asiatic" parts, a Russian visitor wrote with much contempt, except for the "stillness of Oriental despotism," represented by walled houses, narrow empty streets, women wearing hijabs, and idle males.[50]

Colonization brought modern agriculture, urban development, industry, education, and infrastructure. In 1875, a railroad connected Sevastopol to European Russia, making Crimea a Russian alternative to the French Riviera. The Romanovs built residences on the south shore. Aristocrats followed suit. Resort towns such as Yalta sprang up, and by the end of the nineteenth century the south shore had become the vacation spot for the middle class and the literati too. In 1892, Yalta had a population of ten thousand, and the Baedeker guide called it the "most fashionable and expensive of all" Crimean towns, popular for "sea bathing" and the "grape cure." Another type of holistic healing, the "mud cure," with resorts, clinics, and spas, enriched Yevpatoria.[51]

A Riviera it could have been called, but with the standards and services of an underdeveloped country. Said one American tourist in the 1910s: "If that place belonged to us, I guess we would make it the beauty-spot of Europe!"[52] Nonetheless, capitalist development brought a print boom, and for colonized minorities the colonizer's language was a vehicle for accessing contemporary political theory. The anti-colonial Tatar movement in Crimea led to the creation of a party called Vatan, or Fatherland. It remained largely unnoticed by the peninsula's Slavic majority until 1917.

Red Star

Just as in Ukraine, in Crimea the Russian revolutions of 1917 brought terror, civil war, and foreign intervention. As the central Russian government collapsed, the Vatan revolutionaries saw a one-off chance to create a national state for the Tatars. Fighting started between nationalist forces and the Red paramilitary units, proxies of Lenin's government. Neither side shied away from brutality. The bloodbath was brought to an end only by the German occupation in April 1918.

Also as in Ukraine, in Crimea, nationalists, this time Tatar, allied with Germany, and the gambit backfired because they had chosen the losing side in the world war. The fighting that followed after the Germans evacuated at the end of 1918 was worse than what had gone before. The civil war in Crimea was not a bit less horrible than in Ukraine, and for the same reason: while the two major protagonists, the Reds and the Whites, danced a deadly waltz, smaller armies devastated any pockets the big guns missed.[53]

Reds, Whites, Reds, Whites, each with dreadful "counterintelligence" dungeons; neighbors reporting each other out of vengefulness or paranoia; arrests; appeals to strangers in positions of authority; executions, utter unpredictability, despair. Vladimir Nabokov's father, a cabinet minister in a short-lived Crimean liberal government, did not have a single good word for the Whites, citing their lawlessness, anti-Semitism, plundering, searches, arrests, confiscations of private property, and random executions. A small Allied force briefly landed in Crimea, but feeling helpless in the face of an unmanageable civil conflict, quickly evacuated.[54]

In the fall of 1920, Crimea was the last White stronghold still standing. Among other things, that meant it was the last haven for refugees. When the evacuation from Sevastopol began, "nightmarish because of chaos and panic" according to one contemporary observer, it seemed like the definitive end of the old world. In fact it was. On reaching Istanbul, the White generals immediately started a public fight about who had lost Crimea. Among the survivors of the catastrophe, this debate never ceased.[55]

The Bolshevik revolution was the work of two forces, one destructive, the other creative. As it did everywhere else in the Soviet

Union, in Crimea the horrifying terror against the former nobility and bourgeoisie went hand-in-hand with development and social engineering.

For Tatars, that meant nation-building within the Crimean Autonomous Soviet Socialist Republic. The republic was not defined as "Tatar" because they made up only 25 percent of the population (Crimea was 50 percent Russian and Ukrainian; Jews, Greeks, Armenians, Bulgarians, Germans and others accounted for the remaining 25 percent).[56] Yet according to the historian Brian G. Williams, "For all intents and purposes, the Crimean ASSR was, from 1921–1945, established as an unofficial Crimean Tatar republic and the Crimean Tatars were the state-sponsored 'native people.'" Among other progressive achievements was the establishment of universal education in the Tatar language. In 1917, only 17 percent of Tatar girls were enrolled in schools; by 1928, 44.9 percent were. On the destructive side, collectivization, political purges, and, finally, the surreal Great Terror of 1937–1939 hit Tatars as badly as every other group in Crimea. As the Soviet elites were abandoning Marxist cosmopolitanism in favor of pan-Slavic nationalism, the Arabic script that Tatars had traditionally used got changed first to Latin and then, doubling the confusion, into Cyrillic. Planned as a mechanism of reeducation, the change cut off younger people from their heritage.[57]

When Hitler planned the invasion of the Soviet Union and the future disposition of its territories, he gave Crimea a special place. The Crimean mountains *had* been populated by Germanic Goths, and according to the Nazis' research, these Goths were closely related to the Germans living in South Tyrol. This meant, first, that Germans of South Tyrol would be "repatriated" to Crimea after the war, and second, that Tatars of the Crimean mountains would be spared the horrors of racial cleansing because of the possibility that under the veneer of Islamic culture there pulsed noble Aryan blood.

After the war, Crimea was to be renamed Gotenland. Simferopol would become Gotenburg, and Sevastopol would be Theodorich-hafen. The peninsula would become the southernmost Germanic land, the Nazi Riviera.[58]

The German Eleventh Army took Perekop on October 21, 1941. Two and a half years of German occupation followed.[59]

Persistently blind to opportunities for collaboration with the anti-Soviet Russians and Ukrainians, Hitler found collaboration with Muslim peoples ideologically permissible. Tragically, as they had done in 1918, Tatar nationalist activists once again gambled their people's future on an alliance with the wrong side. This mistake was not unique among national liberation movements: Irish nationalists had sided with Germany in World War I.

Out of a population of 218,000, 20,000 Tatars served in the Red Army. Another 20,000 joined "self-defense battalions" directed by the German occupation forces, with the primary mission of hunting down resistance guerrillas in the mountains (at least 20 percent of these guerrillas were Tatars). During the years of occupation, German punitive squads eliminated up to 130,000 Crimean civilians and resistance fighters, including 40,000 Jews; Tatar self-defense units are known to have participated in several massacres.[60]

Historians sympathetic to the Crimean Tatars do not fail to note that a very significant number of Crimean Russians and Ukrainians collaborated with the German occupying force too, both in local administration and volunteer punitive units. Survivors of the occupation have confirmed that. The real dividing line between Tatars and Slavs during the war was not political but economic: Germans let Tatars establish a governing network of so-called Muslim Committees. These committees had very limited functions, such as expanding religious services and establishing a national newspaper and a theater; the most important was the opportunity to regulate economic life in Tatar neighborhoods—an enormous benefit in wartime. Compared with the hand-to-mouth existence of the surviving Slavs, the Tatars' condition of regulated and collective poverty looked like riches.[61]

Once the Red Army returned to the peninsula in May 1944, Stalin ordered every single Tatar deported. They were accused of blanket treason and exiled—in all, about 200,000 people—to Uzbekistan in Central Asia, to spend forty years in a land foreign to them. Other minorities were also kicked out without any explanation: 10,016 Armenians, 12,075 Bulgarians, 14,368 Greeks. All of the 60,000 Crimean Germans had been deported shortly after the war started in 1941. Stalin had decided to make Crimea homogenously Slavic.[62]

What the participants in the Yalta Conference saw ten months later, in February 1945, was a grim, depopulated territory, with Red Army troops lining the roads for heightened security. For many American and British participants, this was their first visit to a territory devastated by war, and they were shocked: "We saw burned-out freight trains, burned-out tanks, and other damaged materiel," Edward R. Stettinius remembered. According to Charles E. Bohlen, the "wreckage Roosevelt saw on the drive hardened his view on Germany. 'I'm more bloodthirsty than a year ago,' he told Stalin when they met." Churchill called Crimea "The Riviera of Hades."[63]

The Kremlin briefly considered creating a Jewish autonomous republic in Crimea, a "Jewish California," an idea already floated in the 1920s. But anti-Semitism, submerged in the 1920s and 1930s, became an official policy of late Stalinism. It was decided that all new settlers would be Ukrainian and Russian.[64]

The majority came from the provinces devastated by war: Russians from the Voronezh, Briansk, Kursk, and Rostov regions; Ukrainians from Kiev, Chernigov, Poltava, and Kamenetz-Podolsk. After the war, 90 percent of the people in Crimea were newcomers. Within a few years, the look of the place had changed. It had become poorer, wanting, confused.[65]

Crimea's history became subject to Slavic revisionism, both Russian and Ukrainian. Both celebrated Crimea as part of "Slavdom," a province of the Kievan Rus'. Most mosques were destroyed, with a few historic ones in tourist centers kept as museums. Agriculture in the mountains was abandoned as too strenuous for Slavs. Tatar villages were razed, leaving abandoned fruit gardens, or *chaeers*, as the only reminders of their occupants' very recent presence. Except for some well-known geographical features, such as capes and mountaintops, Turkic toponyms were either translated into Russian or replaced by something utterly Soviet or distastefully generic.[66]

In 1954, the year of the three hundredth anniversary of the "reunification" of Russia and Ukraine, the then leader of the Soviet Union, Nikita Khrushchev, transferred Crimea from the Russian to the Ukrainian SSR. To Russophiles in Crimea and Russians in general, the transfer was infuriating, yet the insult was not monumental. Khrushchev was not strengthening Ukraine at Russia's expense, he was simply gerrymandering. With the Kremlin power struggle following Stalin's death far from over, he hoped to solidify his power base among the influential Ukrainian apparatchiks who commanded at least 30 percent of the Party Central Committee vote. He also had a soft spot for Ukraine: though not Ukrainian himself, he had been Moscow's viceroy in Kiev. Khrushchev had tried to secure Crimea for Ukraine once before, in 1944 ("Ukraine is in ruins—what if it received Crimea?"). Still, for Russians and Russophiles in Crimea, being transferred to a different republic was not persecution, but it was a degrading objectification. That is how it went down in Russians' memory.[67]

Unlike other Muslim people purged by Stalin in 1944—Chechens, for example—Tatars were never allowed to return: not under Khrushchev, Brezhnev, or Gorbachev. The reason was simple: Crimea's South Shore had become the resort of the dominant Soviet minority, and repatriation of a purged group was a security risk.

As the "All-Union resort," the Black Sea Fleet base, and the vacation spot, the peninsula was in many ways governed directly from Moscow. The umbilical cord was cut only when the Soviet Union unexpectedly fell apart in 1991, and Crimea, by default, remained with Ukraine.

FIVE

Fetish

As I have mentioned, no Crimean product has ever been big internationally, except for the place itself, which is a fetish in several cultures.

The word "fetish" belongs to different narratives—anthropological, sociopolitical, erotic. Definitions vary, but generally speaking, a fetish is something that is assigned a value disconnected from its physical usefulness (a pearl is a good example), but having no inflated meaning outside a certain group of people. Karl Marx, one of the first scholars to start using the term, called the fetishized object a "social hieroglyphic" abounding in "metaphysical subtleties and theological niceties." It is not possible to understand Russian aggression in Crimea without delving into Crimea's status as a fetish.[1]

"To South, to South!"

The famous refrain of Chekhov's *Three Sisters*, from 1900, is "To Moscow, to Moscow, to Moscow!"—the groan of a person stifled by a dull, small-town existence, childishly trusting that a move to the capital will mend broken hearts and restore her sense of purpose. The tension between center and periphery is widely acknowledged as pivotal to Russians; examples, alongside *The Three Sisters*, include Nikolai Nekrasov's canonic juxtaposition of capitals "rocked with thunder / Of orators in wordy feuds" against the "depths of Russia" with its "age-long silence."[2] But another powerful cultural dichotomy, between north and south, is not necessarily noticed.

At around the same time Chekhov wrote *The Three Sisters*, a young Muscovite made an entry in his diary, just as representative as the three sisters' pitiful cry: "Farewell, Moscow!" the boy wrote. "Now to South, to South! To that bright, ever young, ever blooming, beautiful, wondrous South!" Unsurprisingly, he was heading to Crimea—"the sun, the sea," away from "Moscow's mud, cold, and sleet." Since the end of the nineteenth century, numerous texts have echoed the feeling. "Assailed by winter, I withdrew to South," Joseph Brodsky's poem says, his destination "Crimea in January."[3]

On some level, the longing for Crimea of a person living in Russia's hinterlands is not unlike a New Englander's midwinter dream of moving to Florida. In January, the average daytime high temperature in Moscow is eighteen degrees Fahrenheit; in Kiev it is thirty, while in Yalta it is fifty.[4] The only fruit that can be reliably grown around Moscow is an apple the size of a golf ball; in Crimea, mulberries, apricot trees, and grapevines line the streets. Even in the dead of winter, something is in bloom there; the only vegetation thriving at that time of year in Moscow is frost flowers on frozen windows.

But there is more to the Russian fascination with Crimea than a comfortable climate and fresh fruit.

In *Lectures on Russian Literature*, Vladimir Nabokov notes that "Crimea in general, and Yalta in particular, are very beautiful places." Commenting on a line in Chekhov's short story "The Lady with a Dog," set in Yalta, "the sea was of a warm lilac hue with a golden path for the moon," he wistfully writes: "Whoever has lived in Yalta knows how exactly this conveys the impression of a summer evening there." The essay was started twenty years after Nabokov's brief teenage sojourn on Crimea's South Shore, before he was exiled following the revolution, and since then he had traveled extensively along the coasts of France and Italy, in ecosystems similar to southern Crimea and at least as beautiful. For the title of one of the short stories, he nostalgically referenced Crimea as Eden lost, crafting a mesmerizing alliteration "Spring in Fialta"–merging "violet" (*fialka* in Russian) with "Yalta."[5]

There can be little doubt that beauty is a construct. It took our species thousands of years to generally agree that a "warm lilac hue" is more attractive than gray and that the "golden path" of the moon has value beyond the volume of light it adds to navigation, fishing, and war. But again, there is more to the Crimea myth than beauty.

Crimea as a Russian national fetish has layers ranging from spiritual—imperial pride, accumulated sacrifice, accrued effort—to physical. In a materially and emotionally poor country, the physicality of Crimean products carried the whiff of the dolce vita: peaches tender to the touch, sweet tomatoes, fragrant wines—sherry (called by its original Spanish name, *jerez*); madeira; port; moscato; champagne (infringement of the French trademark nonchalantly dismissed). The famously aromatic Sinap apples started to be brought by land-carriage to Moscow and St. Petersburg in the 1790s; two centuries later, people still bring them home from their Crimean vacations. Yet nothing exemplifies the fetishization of Crimea more than the "Koktebel rocks."[6]

Koktebel is a seaside location in eastern Crimea. At the end of the nineteenth century, before the Russian literati colonized it, it was a simple Bulgarian village on a picturesque but not exactly breathtaking bay. Many are deceived by its French-sounding name (*côte de bel? coq de belle?*), but only because they want to be. "Koktebel" comes from Tatar and means Gray Hills. The exact path of the transformation that made Koktebel a cult destination is a separate subject; here, let's look at the end product.[7]

In Chekhov's time, Russians compared Koktebel favorably with Greece, Alicante in Spain, and Italy's Amalfi Coast. This was not totally wrong, as arid Mediterranean coasts have bays much like Koktebel, but still an exaggeration. Koktebel would have been at best mediocre in, say, Peloponnesus. In the Russian empire, it stood out because it was one of the few corners in that uncomfortably northern country that even resembled Greece. By the 1960s, Koktebel had become the place to visit in summer, a combination of artists' colony, playground of the rich, and backpackers' camp—Provincetown, St. Bart's, and South Beach all in one, celebrated in dozens of poems from Marina Tsvetaeva to Brodsky.[8]

Koktebel stands at the foothills of a dead volcano, and the peculiarities of the local currents and seabed put its bay on the receiving end of an underwater bounty, as each storm delivers tens of thousands of semiprecious pebbles of volcanic origin—green, pink, red, yellow, sometimes blue, and called by different names—jasper, agate, chalcedony, carnelian, sardonyx. Usually a beautiful stone collected from the beach loses most of its attractiveness when it dries, its brilliant colors when wet fading like a dead fish. Not so with Koktebel rocks.

On some level, Koktebel rock hunting is similar to collecting shells on Sanibel Island in Florida—but not really. Normally, gathering shells (or rocks) is largely a matter of taxonomy, and for a collector, Sanibel Island is simply the best hunting ground for a wide variety of interesting specimens, a matter of practicality and convenience. With Koktebel rocks, the thing that matters is the origin, not the quality of the specimen. You could have found a brighter jasper elsewhere, but it would be just a rock.

Harvested, transported, kept as family heirlooms, cherished in almost a religious way, Koktebel rocks become talismans of a better, higher world. The cult of collecting was reported as early as the 1890s; by the 1950s, the "colored beaches" of Koktebel had become famous (of course, by now decades of overharvesting have bleached a lot of the color from the Koktebel beach).[9]

Koktebel got a mythologized patron, the poet and artist Maksimillian Voloshin (1877–1932), whose diary entry ("To South! To South!") I quoted a few pages ago. Definitely not a first-tier or second-tier poet, and perhaps worse as an artist, fondly remembered by fans for hundreds of watercolor views of the bay from every possible angle, Voloshin was Koktebel's genius loci. Referred to as Max (the nickname intentionally "Western"), he maintained a salon that later, when times turned hard with the civil war, became a hostel for Russian literati. Inexplicably, he lived through revolution, civil war, and terror unscathed.

Over the years, Voloshin gave shelter and food to hundreds of people. Eventually, an invitation to spend a month at Voloshin's became a definitive sign that one had made it in Moscow's literary and artistic world. Yet his transformation from mere host into Koktebel's patron saint is telling. The whole area became perceived as a territory of singular qualities, largely immune to state meddling, something resembling a safe magical forest in a tale by J. R. R. Tolkien. Max was eccentric, loud, larger than life, and he regarded his village as a sovereign realm. He walked around Koktebel barefoot, in a nightgown, holding an oversized staff—an earthy figure of magical powers.[10]

In the past fifty years, Russian academic hagiography of Voloshin and other literary and artistic figures of the Russian "Silver Age" who happened to reside or visit in the Koktebel area has become amazingly rich. V. P. Kupchenko, for example, a philologist, had spent thirty-four years constructing a day-to-day chronicle of

Voloshin's life, a rare level of attention for any cultural icon. All of the scholarly volumes, conferences, shows, and readings are more a monument to their authors than to their subjects. They also celebrate a fetish—the Crimean peninsula's Mediterranean corner.[11]

Romanticism and Orientalism

In Crimea, the Russian encountered an element he had not likely seen before: the sea. Similarly, living in country that was flat or (barely) rolling, in Crimea he met earth in an intriguing incarnation: mountains.

The empire conquered the mountains and the seacoasts at the time when European Romantics were busy reinventing both. Before that, a cliff had been either an annoying hindrance or a natural foundation for a castle, not something "beautiful." The beach was where fishing boats moored, gulls littered, and winds howled. It was the Romantics who discovered these places as aesthetic experiences. When the Polish national poet Adam Mickiewicz, who visited the peninsula in 1825, published his Crimean Sonnets, out of eighteen poems, six were about bays and beaches, six glorified mountaintops and cliffs, and five sang of ruins.[12] For educated Russians arriving in Crimea, the new domain came with a prefabricated mood.

To Russian visitors from the north, the Black Sea seemed like an outlet to a freer world. Their national poet, Alexander Pushkin, dubbed it the "free element" in a canonic poem. The poem's story is, in fact, deeply unpatriotic: the narrator, like Pushkin in real life, plans to escape Russia by crossing the sea, and fails.[13]

The Black Sea fixation looks strange, as the imperial capital, St. Petersburg, sits on a seacoast too. But by the early nineteenth century (Pushkin wrote his poem in 1824), the shores of the Baltic Sea had been secured by the Russian state, and its traffic was diligently monitored by the police, the customs service, and the navy. Across the sea from St. Petersburg was a Russian protectorate,

Finland. A rebel hoping for escape might have said, "Thanks for nothing, Baltic, you are about as free as I am."

But in the south, the state had not had time to build up its controls. Mikhail Lermontov's "Taman," set on the desolate shores of the Sea of Azov, romanticizes a couple of young and attractive partners in crime, "honest smugglers," as Lermontov calls them (the woman tries drowning the narrator after he discovers what their family business is). The same story mentions a local beauty who had eloped to Turkey across the sea with a Crimean boatman.[14] (Lermontov visited Taman in 1837, at the time of the first Tatar exodus.)

Only a totalitarian state could close coasts that porous. In the USSR, Crimea acquired a new quality—that of a frontier, tantalizingly close to "abroad." The coast became the Black Sea equivalent of the Berlin Wall, from which one occasionally might spot NATO warships teasing the Soviets from the safety of international waters.

Crimea was among the oldest civilizations Russia conquered. The first time Moscow is mentioned in a chronicle is 1147; by then, the Crimean town of Feodosia was fifteen centuries old. To Russians, the cradle of their civilization lies in the eastern Mediterranean—Greece, Palestine, Asia Minor—lands of antiquity and early Christianity. Crimea was the bridge to all that. The prince of the Kievan Rus' who would "baptize" Russia, Vladimir, converted to Orthodox Christianity in Chersonesus, now a suburb of Sevastopol. After Greek myths reached the Russians during the Enlightenment, they were delighted to discover that Crimea and the adjoining Black Sea coasts figure prominently in the stories of Iphigeneia, the Argonauts, and Achilles. Even before setting foot in Crimea, Catherine the Great reimagined the peninsula as a continuation of ancient Greece. That tradition is alive and well two hundred fifty years later.[15]

Pushkin wrote about the green waves of the sea "kissing Taurida," for good measure throwing in an imaginary sighting of the "demi-goddess" Nereid. But Pushkin lived in the age of Romanticism, and for a Romantic pretty much everything came with a classical allusion. A century later, however, in a very different voice, Osip Mandelshtam called Crimean vineyards "Hellenic art in rocky Taurida" and alluded to "Bacchus rites" (nothing but a euphemism for "binge drinking").[16]

Unlike Pushkin, Joseph Brodsky was able to emigrate, but before he did, stifled by the state like Pushkin, he sought refuge in Crimea, again like Pushkin, and reimagined it as a Greco-Roman haven. Brodsky comes not to Yalta but to the "shores of Pontus that does not freeze." He celebrates Christmas in a "tavern"; a random companion in the bar has a "Levantine" face; the bartender circles the room like a "young dolphin"; the steamboats in the harbor are "soiled ichthyosaurs."[17]

Crimea's exoticism made it an ideal setting for Romantic melodrama. Having visited the khans' palace, Pushkin wrote a narrative poem, "The Fountain of Bakhchisaray"—a racy story about passion, betrayal, and vengeance in a harem.[18] The fountain in question is a beautiful mid-eighteenth-century artwork. A cascade carved of white marble belongs to the category of *Selsibil*, the mythical Islamic wellspring of life. Pushkin renamed it the Fountain of Tears. Since then, the poem has inspired an opera and a ballet, and the bust of Pushkin placed next to the fountain itself in the Bakhchisaray palace could be a perfect cover image for a new edition of Edward Said's *Orientalism*.

After "The Fountain of Bakhchisaray," Crimea became for Russian artists what Egypt and the Levant were to their French and Italian contemporaries. As Said put it, they were reinventing the "Orient" through "*positional* superiority, which puts the Westerner in a whole series of possible relationships with the Orient without ever losing him the relative upper hand." Another Crimea testimony from Vladimir Nabokov: "The whole place seemed completely foreign; the smells were not Russian, the sounds were not Russian, the donkey braying every evening just as the muezzin started to chant from the village minaret (a slim blue tower silhouetted against a peach-colored sky) was positively Baghdadian."[19]

Almost every major Russian author of the twentieth century contributed to the collective portrayal of Crimea. Aleksandr Kuprin reimagined the sleepy community of Greek fishermen in the village of Balaclava as descendants of giants, the Laestrygonians of Homer's *Odyssey*. Aleksandr Grinevsky, a favorite companion of several generations of Soviet young adults, writing under a foreign-sounding pen name, Grin, disguised Crimea as a foreign country in a series of action-packed novellas, of which *The Scarlet Sails* is the most popular (and the tackiest). Consistently developing an imagined land around the fair cities of Liss and Zurbagan, the series was later affectionately dubbed "Grinland." The sentimental Konstantin Paustovsky lovingly created a Crimea of abandonment, melancholy, and mystery (unkind reviewers called him delusional for writing about Sevastopol as if it were Marseilles).[20]

As late as the 1950s, books were published on contemporary travels in the Crimean mountains on a par with the Caucasus and Central Asia. With the coasts processed and overdeveloped, Russians wanted to know that some parts of the peninsula remained as exotic, wild, and mysterious as the Pamir Mountains. Joseph Brodsky's narrative poem "Homage to Yalta" is set in the wintery mists of Crimea's South Shore—as if his home city of St. Petersburg (Leningrad at the time) were not sufficiently gloomy to accommodate a murder story.[21]

In the mainland Russian view, the Romantic hero, call him Byronic or demonic, suited Crimea. Look at the narratives woven around the true stories of Crimea at the time of revolution and civil war, 1917–1920.

It happened that in the fall of 1920, Crimea became the last European territory of the former empire to which the Whites still clung. The evacuation of Sevastopol that November was the definitive conclusion of the civil war, ultimate victory for the Reds, ultimate catastrophe for the Whites. Soldiers of the defeated army and civilians of the failed society boarded steamboats in panic, losing track of family and friends, sometimes forever. Horses abandoned by cavalrymen plunged into the sea, following them, apparently also feeling that the separation was final; unable to take the reality of departure, a number of officers shot themselves on deck amid the howling crowds.

Soviet culture treated this exodus with surprising respect. Instead of portraying it as a flight of the low-life scum who got what they richly deserved, Soviet narratives focused on the tragic nature of the human condition—duty, allegiance, and choice—in Vladimir Mayakovsky's words, "yesterday's Russians, tomorrow's refugees." Even more surprising is the representation of the Whites' commander-in-chief, Baron Pyotr Wrangel. Typically, in Red vernacular, Wrangel is "the Black Baron"; but not in November 1920 in Sevastopol. In Mayakovsky's narrative poem, the doomed general is the last to evacuate Sevastopol, as the captain of a perishing ship, and he says his goodbyes to the country he leaves behind kneeling publicly, in the seaport, with bullets whizzing by.[22] Ironically, this grudging admiration comes from the man Stalin called the "best and brightest poet of the Soviet era."

In the words of Osip Mandelshtam, the exodus of 1920 provided Crimea with a permanent "guilty look." Guilt coupled with nostalgia became the emotional core of Mikhail Bulgakov's play *Beg* (Flight), which became a cult phenomenon for its cinematographic rendition in 1970. One could call it a Russian *Gone With the Wind*, a sentimental snapshot of a civilization cut short. *Flight* is a love story, but it starts with the evacuation of Sevastopol in 1920, and one of the protagonists is a White general. Bulgakov's Roman Khludov is based on a real-life character—another Crimean "demon," General Yakov Slashchov (1885–1929).[23]

Thirty-five in 1920, Slashchov was so critical to the defenses of Crimea that Wrangel awarded him the honorific last name "Krymsky," and the town of Yalta made Slashchov an honorary citizen. A gifted strategist, he was also a brutal warlord and a maverick. An American military observer hitching a ride with Slashchov reported to Washington that the general's adjutant "was practically unconscious . . . as he was suffering from a severe head wound he had received the previous day. This is the third adjutant General Slashchev [*sic*] has had in as many months, the first having been killed outright and the second having died of wounds; in both cases the general was within a few feet when the accident occurred. The previous day a shell had landed beneath the general's horse but had not exploded. The general attributed his luck to a large black crow, which, with two ducklings of which he is very fond, shared the front seat of the automobile with a very plump young lieutenant who had given up skirts for red breeches and Hussar boots, and never stirred without rifle and revolver."[24] (The latter misogynistic description refers to Slashchov's wartime mistress.)

As described by witnesses, the flight of the Whites from Odessa and Novorossiysk was just as brutal, chaotic, and inhumanely final, but what remains of history is a story, and in the contemporary narrative it is the evacuation of Sevastopol that concludes the Russian Armageddon of 1917–1920.

"Good Life"

The origins of the town of Yalta are modest and unclear. It may have started as a Greek fishing village or a tiny Genoese post, but it cannot be found on a map until the mid–nineteenth century, when it was incorporated. At that point, Yalta was a sad little affair: in the words of contemporaries, a "village of some forty white houses, forming a single street," an "abode of poor fishermen," surrounded by "extensive woods." Its industry was a handful of boats harvesting oysters. Half a century later, it was an established resort with all the expected "European" amenities, including snow and ice delivered from the mountains by the Tatars.[25]

Romanticism revolutionized this inconspicuous coastal town. Before the age of Byron, when natural beauty was worth nothing, settlements were built where they were built because the location was either secure or profitable, preferably both. People started coming to Yalta because that was what the upper classes were doing in Europe—going to small coastal places to relax in style and meet other people who also relaxed in style. Yalta got incorporated because it had potential for the new resort industry.

A visitor in the 1840s wrote: "Nothing can be more charming than the sight of that white Ialta [*sic*], seated at the head of a bay like a beautiful sultana bathing her feet in the sea, and sheltering her fair forehead from the sun under rocks festooned with verdure. Elegant buildings, handsome hotels, and a comfortable, cheerful population, indicate that opulence and pleasure have taken the town under their patronage; its prosperity, indeed, depends entirely on the travellers who fill its hotels for several months of the year." A Western writer called it "one of the most charming places in Europe for the invalid."[26]

After the Crimean War, not just the tsar but his brothers, uncles, and cousins thought it patriotic to build estates on the Russian Riviera. In 1867, the passengers of the first American cruise ship ever to visit the Black Sea were given a tour of several royal residences and an audience with Emperor Alexander II and his wife. One of the passengers was Mark Twain, who registered the imperial couple's strong desire to impress the American "innocents" with "handsome" gardens, "grand old groves," and "Grecian architecture."[27]

Another visitor observed in 1874: "For twelve miles after leaving Yalta, there is a succession of highly-cultivated estates, and the palaces attached to them glimmer white upon the mountain side. More delightful abodes it would be impossible for the imagination to picture. One would almost believe that neither sorrow nor sickness could enter their doors; and yet, if it were so, how hard it would be to leave them for the grave!" Among the last generation of the Romanovs, almost every member of the royal family had a residence in Crimea, and in 1919, when the survivors were leaving Yalta on the British battleship *Marlborough*, the separation was hard indeed.[28]

The scenery of the South Shore has been variously compared to Amalfi and the Maritime Alps; one group of visitors agreed that "never, on the coasts of Italy, Spain, or Northern Africa had we seen such a combination of the magnificent and the beautiful, united with such a glow of colour, as on this seaboard." Another visitor argued that even Switzerland could scarcely compare with the "tremendous granite precipices" of South Shore. To Mark Twain, a "beautiful spot" of "Yalta, Russia" resembled a "vision of the Sierras."[29]

But now let us listen to another witness: Anton Chekhov, who very unhappily spent the last years of his life in Yalta, exiled there by tuberculosis. Visitors and vacationers admired the South Shore's looks; Chekhov abhorred its soul. Yalta, he wrote in a letter, "is a cross that not everyone can bear. It abounds in drabness, slanders, intrigue and the most shameless calumny."[30]

Chekhov's iconic Yalta story, "The Lady With the Dog," portrays Yalta as a place of one-night stands, a banal seaside resort where people shed their inhibitions with the full knowledge that this would have no consequences for their real life up north. When Anna Sergeevna tells Gurov that he will stop respecting her now, he finds this so obvious that he just keeps eating a watermelon. There are several shockers in the story, and one is that a trite vacation dalliance inexplicably grows into something more consequential.

When this realization hits him, Gurov blurts out to an acquaintance, If you only knew what a remarkable woman I met in Yalta! The acquaintance replies: You were right about the fish they served today—it was *not* fresh. He knows exactly what kind of encounters occur in Yalta and dismisses Gurov's exclamation as a bout of sentimentality brought on by excessive drinking (and possibly by the bad fish).[31]

In a less famous story, Chekhov identifies Crimea, and Yalta in particular, as a destination for Russian middle-class female sex tourists, hiring Tatar escorts for the duration of their stay so as to brag about the adventures back home. A contemporary conservative Russian journalist lamented the "loose" morals of women vacationers in Yalta, the town "not a resort, but a school of seduction."[32]

Chekhov would have been annoyed to learn that for more than a century, Yalta has been his shrine, with a museum, conferences, readings, and theater festivals. Meeting in Yalta in 2009 to negotiate an energy deal amid an atmosphere of bonhomie and flirtation, Vladimir Putin and the then Ukrainian prime minister Yulia Tymoshenko announced they would be having a tête-à-tête dinner. "We will be discussing Chekhov," Putin playfully told the reporters.[33]

Sevastopol

To a person not fixed on politics or war, Sevastopol may look like an utterly delightful city. Profoundly maritime, it rides the hills above a calm narrow bay where sharp warships sit at anchor.

The bay is sometimes called a fjord, though specialists insist it is a ria, a drowned river valley, just like another mariners' haven in the eastern Mediterranean, the Bay of Kotor in Montenegro. In Sevastopol, the river is the Chornaya, nowadays an insignificant affair barely twenty miles long.

Sevastopol means August City. Founded in 1783 on Catherine the Great's orders, it was meant to be the military springboard of

Russian imperial expansion into Ottoman lands. Ironically, it became famous for the 349-day siege it suffered during the Crimean War. Habitually calculating patriotism through loss, Russians still seem proud that 127,500 of their compatriots died there in 1854 and 1855. Another way of looking at it is that the sailors and soldiers had no choice: they were at the mercy of their commanders, who were at the mercy of Nicholas I, the Iron Tsar.[34]

In Russia, the person who put Sevastopol on the literary map was Leo Tolstoy, a veteran of the siege. His fictionalized memoir *The Sebastopol Sketches* made him a national celebrity. Already with the first installment of the work published, Tsar Alexander II saw the propaganda value of the piece and ordered it translated into French for dissemination abroad. That made the young author very happy. Compared with Tolstoy's later novels, *The Sebastopol Sketches* hasn't aged well, possibly because this is not a heartfelt book. As the twenty-six-year-old Tolstoy's Sevastopol diaries reveal, not heartache but ambition drove him at the time. Making a name as an author was just an alternative to two other grand plans—founding a new religion and creating a mathematical model for winning in cards (his losses during the siege were massive even for a rich person). Yet the book's message lives: Sevastopol is the City of Russian Glory. What also likely played a role was that nineteenth-century Russians needed to put an ethnic stamp on the still somewhat alien Crimean shore.[35]

Twelve years after the siege, Mark Twain noted that "Pompeii is in good condition compared to Sevastopol. Here, you may look in whatsoever direction you please, and your eye encounters scarcely any thing but ruin, ruin, ruin!" Two years later, an Englishwoman reported: "Not a single ship in the harbor, and all the forts and fortifications—indeed, the whole town on the south side—almost one mass of ruins. The *débris* of houses, forts, and barracks remain just as they were left in 1856, and a population which then amounted, it is said, to 60,000, has been reduced to 5,500!"[36]

The poet Anna Akhmatova spent her childhood summers in the vicinity. The narrator of her poem about Sevastopol picks "French bullets, like others pick mushrooms." Imagining herself a tsarina, the girl dispatches "six battleships and six gunboats" to protect the area's bays.[37]

During World War II, history repeated itself: Sevastopol was put through another siege. On June 22, 1941, it became the first Soviet city bombed by the Germans, and it was the call from the commander of the Black Sea Fleet that alerted Moscow to the catastrophe. In November, after the Red Army evacuated the rest of the peninsula, the siege of Sevastopol continued for eight more months. A German soldier remembered: "Numerous Russians lay wounded, scattered among the vineyards under a merciless, scorching sun. There was no water available to them where they lay, and they were quickly overcome with a sense of apathy as they lay waiting to die on the open ground."[38]

Soviet generals seem to have been touched by the tragic continuity, sort of a deadly noblesse oblige. In 1941–1942, Sevastopol "fought heroically," "true to its military heritage," Stalin's chief of general staff wrote. The minister of the navy reported that the city stood like an "invincible rock" where "real life heroes shed blood for the Fatherland" next to the ghosts of Tolstoy's "no less dear and familiar heroes."[39]

In both wars, Sevastopol was a fortress, holding off the enemy for months and refusing to surrender, not the base of aggressive naval operations envisioned at its birth. If Sevastopol is the "City of Russian Glory," its glory is tragic. "If we are told to die fighting, we will die fighting unquestioningly," its story seems to tell us. This is exactly the kind of pledge the Leviathan of the Russian state likes to hear.

But according to Russian Orthodoxy, Sevastopol is sacred grounds twice over. In 988, Prince Vladimir, the ruler of Kievan Rus', converted to Christianity in Chersonesus; returning to Kiev, he made Orthodoxy the state religion—as tradition says, converting the rest of the country "by sword and fire."[40]

In the mid–nineteenth century, local clergy tried making Crimea a "Russian Athos," intending to steal the clout of the original Mount Athos, an autonomous theocracy on the Chalkidiki Peninsula in northern Greece, which had traditionally been the center of Eastern Orthodox mysticism. Crimea's South Shore resembled the Holy Mountain in looks; some Christian sites on the peninsula *were* old; Christians and Muslims alike venerated a number of locales for their alleged paranormal qualities.

To that purpose, several monasteries got fixed or built—St. George's near Balaklava, Dormition in Bakhchisaray, Inkerman off Sevastopol, Cosmas' and Damian's deep in the mountains. For several years, the rebranding seemed to work, attracting Orthodox pilgrims. What unexpectedly killed the project was technological progress: steamships allowed a pilgrim to reach the real Athos from any Black Sea port in only two or three days.[41]

The Black Sea Fleet

One can't tell the story of the Crimean War or World War II without Sevastopol. But take out the Russian Black Sea Fleet, and nothing in the bigger picture changes. Here we come to one of the many paradoxes of Russian history: although it is a staple of Russian state mythology, and a powerful presence in literature, art, and politics, the Russian navy has very little to boast of in terms of battles won and enemy fleets destroyed. To this day, its biggest feat remains its tragic journey around Europe, Africa, and Asia in 1904–1905 to the Sea of Japan, where it was decimated by the Japanese navy in the infamous Battle of Tsushima.[42]

The navy is the "favorite child of Peter the Great," because he built it from scratch, first by learning for himself how to build warships on the wharfs of Holland and England. The new capital, St. Petersburg, was conceived as a glorified base for his favorite child. Yet despite all the effort, cost, sweat, and blood spilled, the Russian navy remained more a meme than a real thing, more romantic than sensible, more patriotic than practical.

Russia's geographical limits make a big navy an expensive toy: few warm-water ports, too many inner seas, and a total inability to move a fleet quickly from one theater to another. A winning weapon for Russia is aircraft and missile, not cruiser and submarine.

The folly is particularly apparent in the south. The Sea of Azov, the Black Sea, and the Mediterranean are like three nesting dolls. An unfriendly force can lock each one of them shut—the Sea of Azov at the Strait of Kerch, the Black Sea at the Bosporus and the Dardanelles, the Mediterranean at Gibraltar. Short of an unimaginable collapse of the West, there is no geostrategic situation that could give the Russian Black Sea Navy unhindered access to the Atlantic.

During the Crimean War, the Russian fleet, blockaded in Sevastopol by the British and the French, became a heroic sitting duck. The Russians ended up scuttling their ships to prevent the Allies from moving into the harbor. In 1918, to keep Germans from capturing it, Russians scuttled the fleet in Novorossiysk. In 1942, abandoning Sevastopol, the Soviets scuttled the fleet again. One could say that the Russian Black Sea Fleet kills itself with shocking readiness: suicide may be its most effective tactic. The Monument to the Scuttled Ships at the entrance to Sevastopol harbor, a tasteless column awkwardly stuck into a pyramid of rocks, has been a symbol of the city since 1905. The bronze eagle on top, crowning the column with a laurel wreath, looks eternally perplexed, as if it were not sure what exactly the monument celebrates.

The admirals who presided over the defense of Sevastopol in 1853–1856, Vladimir Kornilov, Pavel Nakhimov, and Vladimir Istomin, all killed during the siege and buried in the Admirals' Vault in St. Vladimir Cathedral in Sevastopol, entered the pantheon of Russian military geniuses. At least five Russian ships have borne Nakhimov's name. In 1944, Joseph Stalin established the Nakhimov Medal for sailors, the Nakhimov Order for officers, and Nakhimov schools for young cadets.

As a fetish, Crimea appeals to every ideological camp. Members of the liberal intelligentsia are attracted to Chekhov, Koktebel, and Brodsky, while the far right, despising Koktebel as decadent, idolizes Sevastopol and the Black Sea Fleet.

As Russia's fixation focuses on Crimea as an assemblage of inanimate objects (relics of the past; urban structures; rock, sea, beach) and memories (people and narratives), the agency of the actual people living on the peninsula fades to the background. In Russian eyes, the peninsula has little function except as an object of desire. The Tatars' legacy and current strife are ignored, Ukraine's are ridiculed, and the Crimean Russophiles are seen only as hostages Russia had to rescue.

SIX

The Takeover

The native Crimean cast of the 2014 crisis is usually described as Russians, Ukrainians, and Tatars, as if national identities were as distinct as military insignia, superseding generation and class. No matter how you define "ethnicity" ("language," "blood," "tradition"), it alone could never have determined how Crimeans reasoned and acted during the crisis. No cultural group on the peninsula was monolithic.

Native Cast

The pending change on the peninsula jeopardized the rights and privileges of some and promised to expand them for others. Russia was not exactly an unknown quantity; on the peninsula, it had a presence, a reputation, and a history. Similarly, Ukraine, which was on the way to losing Crimea, was not a paragon of peace and prosperity. Wages in Ukrainian Crimea were among the lowest in Europe: they averaged $300 a month, versus $700 in the rest of Ukraine, $1,200 in Russia, and $1,500 in Poland. In theory, at least,

Crimea was moving from a poorer community to a richer one in becoming part of Russia, with higher living standards, more jobs, and more upward mobility.[1]

For Crimean Russophiles, a group containing many ethnic and cultural backgrounds, reunification with Russia had been a priority for twenty years. In 1994, a democratically elected president of Crimea, Yury Meshkov, actually attempted secession, but Yeltsin's Kremlin brushed him off; the Russian economy at the time was in shambles, Yeltsin needed U.S. aid, and he did not want to jeopardize his good standing with President Clinton. Also, Moscow was fighting a war in Chechnya and had neither the resources nor the willpower for a conflict with Ukraine.[2]

Nationalist ideologues and populist politicians in mainland Russia, meanwhile, never gave up their claims on Crimea and the "City of Russian Glory." Unspecified but not insignificant sums of private money fed Russophile cultural and political nongovernmental organizations on the peninsula. An American visitor to the city in the 1990s noted "its passionate Russian-ness, its stunned refusal to acknowledge the collapse of the Soviet Union." Local newspapers were called *Glory to Sevastopol* and *The Motherland Flag*.[3]

Crimean Russophiles hoped reunification would bring structure and order. A Russian anthropologist has called Crimea an "oasis of conservatism," a condition originating in the service industry built around government residences, in the power of the military, and in the prejudices and insecurities of Russian and Ukrainian settlers now occupying Tatars' land. Vladimir Putin's system of governance was built on conservative values. The appeal of order, even if not necessarily coupled with law, increased dramatically after the extremist wing of the Euromaidan triggered violent clashes all over Ukraine.[4]

On the eve of the crisis, Ukraine had eighteen thousand troops stationed in Crimea; Russia around sixteen thousand. Apart from their strictly military role, Russian garrisons on the peninsula were important strategically as close-knit expatriate communities. Sailors, soldiers, and airmen came and went, drafted and then discharged, but their commanding officers stayed longer, often marrying and starting families in Crimea. These military communities were magnets for Russophile groups. There can be little doubt that Moscow secret services had been nurturing them. A prime example is a Sevastopol bikers' club with the tacky name Night Wolves, which would gain notoriety in the 2014 events.[5]

The pro-Kiev minority in Crimea was no less diverse than the Russophiles. These groups included enterprises owned by or financially dependent on mainland Ukraine; state workers with vested interests in the preservation of the existing order; idealistic patriots; multicultural liberals preferring Ukrainian chaos to Russian authoritarianism; and, last but not least, Tatars who rightfully believed that their autonomy would suffer under Russian rule.

Tatars

Crimean Tatars were allowed to begin the painful process of repatriation from Central Asia only when the Soviet state grew weak, in the late 1980s. Their movement, led by Mustafa Dzhemilev, was never encouraged by Moscow or Kiev. A comrade of Andrei Sakharov, Dzhemilev came from the humanistic intelligentsia tradition. He preached nonviolence. He had in mind something more than physical return to the Green Isle: his plan was to reinvent the Crimean Tatar nation.

Western and Russian historiography traditionally maintained that Crimean Tatars had originated in the Golden Horde of Genghis Khan, with the Crimean Khanate forming the "last Mongol outpost." The new generation of Tatar intelligentsia, raised and educated in exile, decided on a new interpretation of their origins: yes, they were related to Mongols, but also to every other group in Crimea's early history, including Huns, Alans, Avars, Goths, Greeks. They rejected the label "Crimean Tatars" as a colonialist misnomer, saying they were simply *Crimeans*, Kirim, the sum of the peninsula's history, not a mere part of it, unlike Russians and Ukrainians. Anthropologically, this claim was impossible to verify or refute. Intellectually, it was challenging; politically it was confrontational, naming Tatars as the only true indigenous Crimean nation.[6]

In 1979, just 5,000 Tatars lived in Crimea; by the spring of 1987, their numbers had grown to 17,500; by the end of 1990, to 100,000. By 1996, 240,000 had returned, and they made up 9.1 percent of the Crimean population. After that, mass repatriation stalled.[7]

It was estimated that 500,000 Crimean Tatars lived in the former USSR, mostly in Central Asia. Half of them chose to stay where Stalin's deportation had brought them fifty years earlier. Of course, they made that choice for a reason.

From the start, the authorities—first Soviet, then Ukrainian—intended to keep the return migration limited to Crimea's northern steppe area, excluding Tatars from the South Shore with its prime property, resorts, and military installations. In that they largely succeeded. The Soviet and Ukrainian central governments refused to provide any legal framework regulating property rights and residence permits for the repatriates. Individual settlers' fates, therefore, were decided locally: arbitrarily and meanly.[8]

Crimean authorities, citing a not unreasonable need to identify legitimate repatriates, demanded proof of their origins. In practice, however, the requirement was absurd. The repatriate had to have a proof of his or his ancestors' legal address as of May 18, 1944. But many Tatar families had left their homes without any documents.

Furthermore, for any Tatars who had such documentation, it was a curse. The Crimean authorities sent them back to the rural areas where the majority of Tatars had come from in 1944. Fifty years earlier, their families had been farmers, but now these educated people, born and raised in urban areas of Soviet Central Asia, were "repatriated" to the countryside, where they were not prepared to make a living. This was an appalling case of discrimination: people of other ethnic backgrounds could settle wherever they wanted in Crimea.[9]

There was no concept of restitution. Tatars returning to Crimea had to build their lives from scratch. Unsurprisingly, the building lots they were able to secure tended to be horrible. Ethnic harassment was common, extortion endemic. In many cases, unable to get any approval from the town hall, Tatars settled as squatters. Just 20 percent of their settlements had electricity. Despite the authorities' precautions and Dzhemilev's efforts to advocate nonviolence, the early 1990s saw bitter clashes between settlers and Slavs, the latter often supported by corrupt and brutal police.[10]

To Moscow's relief, after 1991 the Kirim became Kiev's burden. Ukraine tried to engage Russia and Uzbekistan, holding them responsible for the Tatars' plight and asking for financial help, but the request was brushed off. The only stable foreign donor for the Kirim was the Ottomans' successor state, Turkey, which pledged about $87 million for home construction and study programs in Turkey for young people. Religious revival got more funding, as numerous foreign Islamic groups donated money to build or restore mosques and start schools and charities.[11]

By the turn of the century, the dust had settled a bit. Dzhemilev's group had negotiated a kind of benign apartheid for the Tatars: they had their own national assembly, the Qurultai, and an executive arm, the Mejlis. For all intents and purposes, these were institutions of self-rule, operating within a perhaps intentionally vague delimitation of power between themselves and the Ukrainian state. Dzhemilev was able to wrest this precariously de facto autonomy from Kiev because Ukrainian leaders intended to use the Crimean Tatars as a counterbalance to the peninsula's Russophiles.

In the absence of any survey data, it is hard to tell what percentage of Tatar settlers found Ukrainian rule in Crimea a lesser evil than Russian rule. A factor to consider is the rise of the Tatar propertied class. Settlers arriving in Crimea in the 1980s were more or less equal; since then, capitalism had created stratification within the community. Svetlana Chervonnaya, a scholar who did fieldwork in Crimea, bitterly commented that after seeing shantytowns next to mansions, she found it "difficult to imagine a united Crimean Tatar nation." Nationalism and identity aside, the Tatar upper class simply could not have risen without integrating with the Crimean economy, which meant collaborating with the Russophile elites. That helped the intercommunal armistice stand.[12]

Agitation

Carelessness, infighting, bad judgment, and corruption had prevented Ukraine from forging a strong military. Counting on exactly that, Vladimir Putin launched a covert takeover operation that precluded bloodshed or the conspicuous use of arms. Putin claimed that he ordered the annexation of Crimea only after the ousting of Viktor Yanukovych, in the small hours of February 23, 2014. This may be true, but some preparations for the takeover must have begun earlier.[13]

Three political goals had to be reached before the military operation began. The Russophiles on the peninsula had to be mobilized; the political establishment of Crimean Tatars had to be neutralized; and world opinion had to be probed for sympathy and prepared for the eventuality.

The casus belli for Crimean separatism was the specter of "Ukrainian fascism." Far-right nationalist groups commanded only marginal support in Ukraine, but their presence in Euromaidan and riots elsewhere suggested a determination and vengefulness lacking in other political forces. The Russophiles in the Crimean government, grassroots activists, and of course Putin's propaganda machine predicted imminent invasion and massacres by "fascists from Western Ukraine."

This catastrophic scenario was far-fetched but not baseless. The Ukrainian far-right parties and militias were already spread too thin throughout Ukraine's core, and there was no way they could seriously threaten Crimea. But, usefully for Putin, they talked a good game. Their bellicose rhetoric, their smug use of Nazi symbols, and their declarations of an all-out war against "Ivans" (*moskaly*) were all real.

All over Ukraine, people died in ambushes, street fighting, and arsons, and although the total casualties probably did not exceed two hundred, rumors increased that number tenfold. In the atmosphere of uncertainty and fear, and with the Ukrainian state collapsing, the idea of seceding from Ukraine and joining Russia was an easy sell to Crimea's majority.

Neutralizing the Tatar leadership was more difficult. Mustafa Dzhemilev warned that Tatars would not accept a referendum at gunpoint. He could not be swayed even when Putin called him personally. But Crimea's new class of Tatar entrepreneurs was less resistant to Moscow's overtures.

The Kremlin asked leaders of the Volga Tatar community to intercede in Crimea, to showcase the benefits of being with Russia. The 2 million Volga Tatars were autonomous within the Russian Federation—the Republic of Tatarstan, centered on its capital, Kazan, a thriving regional metropolis. Predictably, Kazan loyalists failed to persuade Dzhemilev, but their effect on the Crimean Tatar business community was significant.[14]

Russia has 20 million Muslims, more than any other country in Europe, and they make up the country's second-largest religious group after Orthodox Christians. In a new spirit of interfaith cooptation, Putin declared Islam "a striking element of the Russian cultural code, an inalienable, organic part of Russian history." Russia's mainstream Muslim clerics embraced the "harmony and unity" approach. All of that should have at least somewhat alleviated the Crimean Muslims' concerns.[15]

The Kremlin could not possibly have hoped to achieve as much in the outside world. The "Ukrainian fascists" card was hard to play with foreign audiences. First, the threat posed by the Euromaidan far right was largely latent. Second, after the numerous follies of the 2000s—especially its effort to present a brutal war on Chechnya as a defensive battle against terrorists—Putin's propaganda apparatus had zero credibility in the West. Third, mainstream Western media venues, both liberal and conservative, had sided with the Euromaidan from the very beginning. Changing their minds was an impossible task.

But the Kosovo precedent could not be easily dismissed. Military intervention in Kosovo under Bill Clinton, and George W. Bush's blithe sponsorship of Kosovo's independence, now became Moscow's constant source of justification for the impending Crimea takeover.

Just like Crimea, Kosovo had been an autonomous region of a sovereign state, Serbia. If Kosovo had been allowed to secede, Moscow argued, why not Crimea? The difference, said Western commentators, was Serbian atrocities in Kosovo, to which Moscow wryly responded that it did not plan to wait until Ukrainian extremists started massacring the citizens of Sevastopol.[16]

Hybrid Warfare

The peninsula fell under Russian control within three weeks, even though Moscow officially had no troops on the ground. The Kremlin announced that there was no need for them because grassroots Crimean militias were taking over effectively, independently, and bloodlessly. There were, in fact, Russophile militias in Crimea consisting of local volunteers, but they were herded and led by armed strangers, the "little green men." Putin did not admit to using Russian special forces until the first anniversary of the takeover.

Variously called a "stealth invasion," "non-linear war," "hybrid war," "special war," "asymmetric," and "ambiguous" warfare, the strategy would resurface in eastern Ukraine. Based, in the words of Western military analysts, on "deception, deniability and special operations troops mixed with volunteer militias," it was a "new form of warfare that cannot be characterized as a military campaign in the classic sense of the term. The invisible military occupation cannot be considered an occupation by definition."[17]

Russia expert Mark Galeotti provides strong evidence that the "hybrid war" doctrine was conceived at least a year before the actual invasion.[18] That would certainly explain its success in Crimea. This is what happened.

Hardcore nationalist cells on the peninsula, such as the Night Wolves, were called to arms. Presumably, Moscow told them the general plan of the campaign and assigned roles to individual groups. Ways of supplying them with weapons were arranged. A similar process occurred in the regions of mainland Russia that already had nationalistic militias. The Kuban Cossacks were one such group, which crossed into Crimea across the Strait of Kerch in the early days of the campaign.

Russian commandos disrupted cable communications between Ukrainian forces in Crimea and central command in Kiev, while Russian military hackers mounted "denial-of-service attacks" against Ukrainian government and media outlets in cyberspace. Cyber PR professionals, the Kremlin "trolls" in Internet-speak, invaded social networks, mobilizing Crimean separatists and confusing the Ukrainian adversary.

Ukrainian military commanders in Crimea found themselves stalked and threatened, mob-style. When threats did not persuade a Ukrainian commander to desert, defect, or surrender, paramilitary groups like the Night Wolves stepped in. On at least one occasion, they kidnapped a high-ranking Ukrainian general.

At the end of February, Russian marines, paratroopers, and military intelligence special forces began to arrive in Crimea, either undercover via legitimate ports of entry or landing at the Sevastopol naval base or at Russian air force bases in the steppes. After their numbers reached six or seven thousand, Russian commandos blockaded Ukrainian troops in their bases. All strategic locations were occupied. One of the first was Chernomorneftegaz (Black Sea Oil and Gas Company) headquarters and its offshore platforms in the Sea of Azov.[19]

Perhaps the main value of this approach was that Russia's larger strategic plan remained invisible, and every new step took Ukraine by surprise. The biggest feat in this respect was the neutralization of the Ukrainian navy stationed in the Donuzlav lagoon north of Sevastopol. Instead of engaging it in battle or even threatening to, the Russians just sank four of their own older ships at the mouth of the lagoon. No doubt this was also meant as a macabre joke, a reference to the sinking of the Russian fleet during the Crimean War.[20]

To make sure NATO understood the seriousness of Russian intentions, Moscow deployed to Sevastopol an advanced coastal defensive missile system, called Bastion. As Putin put it slyly, "We deployed them so they could be seen clearly from space." The Bastions were a statement. According to foreign experts, the Bastions covered the coast of southern Ukraine, including Odessa, its only major port, and "much of the Black Sea itself." The missiles were thought to be able to select an individual target from a group "even in a jamming environment."[21]

Except for a few half-hearted attempts at resistance, Ukrainian forces gave up Crimea without a fight. On March 21, the Russian flag was raised at 147 Ukrainian military facilities in Crimea and on 54 Ukrainian naval ships, including the nation's lone submarine.[22]

It is important to note that Moscow's spectacular military success in Crimea was explained not by Putin's prowess or Russian strategic ingenuity, but by the tragic disarray of the Ukrainian military on and around the peninsula. The infiltration of the "little green men" could have been prevented, or at least effectively contained, had Ukraine maintained even modestly operational border controls and special forces. The entry points were few and well known. The Strait of Kerch (ferries), and the Perekop Isthmus (trains and automobiles) could have been securely blockaded with just a few hundred determined servicemen. The same goes for the perimeters of Russian air force and navy bases, which received planeloads of "polite soldiers." A combat-ready force of two thousand soldiers might have been all Ukraine needed to deter Russian aggression in Crimea. This should not be too much to ask of a state that, at least on paper, had an army of 130,000.[23]

A lasting lesson from the 2014 takeover of Crimea is that the "new Russian military strategy" can be used only against failing states. In Ukraine, like an opportunistic infection, it finished off a body already eaten up by disease. Putin's is a strategy of vultures, not raptors.

Ascension

With the referendum in progress, on March 11, eighty-five Russian artists and writers published an open letter supporting Putin's policy in "Ukraine and Crimea." One of the signers was long dead and another had not been consulted, but the rest of signatures were real. Many belonged to intellectuals typically described as "pro-Western," including regulars of the Manhattan cultural scene—the pianist Denis Matsuev, conductors Yury Bashmet and Vladimir Spivakov, the dancer Nikolai Tsiskaridze. The father of perestroika and glasnost, Mikhail Gorbachev, called the annexation a "happy event." He was seconded by the head of the House of Romanov in exile, Grand Duchess Maria Vladimirovna.[24]

Russian state-controlled media exploited American involvement, making it sound as if U.S. puppeteers now made every decision for Kiev. TV anchors warned that Ukraine could join NATO at any time. Putin and the Russian street saw eye to eye on many things: Crimea as an imperial fetish, the threat from NATO, U.S. involvement in Kiev and military interventions worldwide. The mood in Russia was one of resurgence and Reconquista.

Despite the international outcry, Crimean polls opened as scheduled on March 16. Many Tatars boycotted an election that they could not sway in any case. The official figures—96 percent saying "yes," with 82 percent turnout—are hard to believe and impossible to verify. Yet observers agree that Crimeans overwhelmingly supported the move. Had the referendum been transparent, with foreign observers present, Crimea would have still voted "yes." It is hard to explain rationally why Putin would not have allowed that.

In the Kremlin on March 18, with much pomp, Putin signed a "treaty of ascension" of Crimea and Sevastopol to Russia. The Republic of Crimea was incorporated as a federal subject of the Russian Federation, and Sevastopol as a federal city. That put the City of the Russian Glory in the same category with Moscow and St. Petersburg, an unprecedented honor, but also an indication that the fortress would now be ruled directly by the Kremlin. Jubilant Russian social networks spat up a patriotic Twitter hashtag, #CrimeaIsOurs (krymnash). This quickly developed into a noun for the ardent supporters of the Russian president (as in "only *krymnashi* will be attending").

Not undeservedly, Vladimir Putin took credit for the "reunification." When he visited Sevastopol on May 9 (not coincidentally, V-Day in the Russian calendar) his theatrical entry into the bay onboard a warship was meant to look like the return of a king.

PART III

Consequences

SEVEN

From Crimea to Donbass

Ninety-two United Nations member states refused to judge Russia's actions in Crimea. The handful of countries that joined Russia in voting against the American-sponsored U.N. resolution to condemn the annexation were either perennially anti-American or eating from Moscow's hand: Armenia, Belarus, Bolivia, Cuba, Nicaragua, North Korea, Sudan, Syria, Venezuela, and Zimbabwe. Their vote was to be expected. But among the countries that either abstained or did not vote were several third-world powerhouses and U.S. allies, including Afghanistan, Argentina, China, India, Iraq, Israel, and Pakistan. All were involved in territorial disputes with other countries; none wanted the West as an arbiter.

In Washington, support for Ukraine immediately became a bipartisan issue. On March 6, the House of Representatives approved $1 billion in financial aid to Kiev by a vote of 385 to 23. The White House introduced sanctions against Russia. Conservatives and liberals alike asked for an even stronger response. Senators John McCain, Lindsey Graham, and Robert Menendez demanded that

Obama send weapons to Ukraine. Nicholas Kristof of the *New York Times* urged the president to act preemptively and start rescuing another post-Soviet nation potentially facing Russian intervention —Moldova.[1]

Within weeks, the Moscow-supported "people's republics" of Donetsk and Luhansk began battling Ukrainian forces. By March 2016, according to U.N. estimates, there were 9,160 deaths.[2]

Russian Volunteers

In neither Ukraine nor Russia are Donetsk and Luhansk referred to as "eastern Ukraine," a broad term that is applicable to several additional provinces. The region is called Donbass.

Donbass stands for "Donetz Coal Basin"—the Donetz a river, and coal the essence of the local economy. Donbass is part of the steppes. It supported no urban centers before the Russian Empire secured it, and no significant towns until coal became an indispensable commodity in the second half of the nineteenth century. Almost every settlement was born as a mining town, and most remain mining towns today. The peak of development happened in the 1920s and 1930s. As a result, the foundations of Donbass social norms and human geography are neither Ukrainian nor Russian, but Soviet, formed by central planning serving the needs of industrialization. Migration of a skilled workforce, establishment of vocational and technical education, city planning—nothing was spontaneous. Donbass is a product of social engineering. Nowadays, its coal deposits depleted and heavy industry outdated, many towns of Donbass resemble former mill towns in the American Northeast: places where economic depression manifests itself in decay, unemployment, poverty, and anger.

The exact mechanism of the separatist insurgency in Donbass is still not known, but it was neither a grassroots revolution, as Moscow claims, nor a conspiracy cooked up in the Kremlin, as Kiev insists.

The overthrown president of Ukraine, Viktor Yanukovych, was from Donbass, and his ouster was a victory of Donbass's nemesis—nationalist Galicia.

The whole of Ukraine was in turmoil between February and April of 2014, and at first, the rallies in Donbass did not look so different from those roaring in Lviv or Odessa. When pro-Russian activists in Donetsk and Luhansk proclaimed "people's republics," it sounded almost like comic relief. It took the Kremlin to turn a soap opera into a war.

It does not look as if Moscow planned the infiltration of eastern Ukraine as a smooth continuation of the expansion begun in Crimea. Nor was it attempting, as it is often argued, to create a land corridor to Crimea along the coast of the Sea of Azov. No Russian traffic there would ever be safe from Ukrainian paramilitary attacks. Most likely, Putin opted for the escalation because he was angered by the U.S. reaction to the "ascension" of Crimea into Russia, yet scornful of the first round of sanctions. Indeed, in the spring of 2014, they did not bite. Like a willful cat testing the limits of what he can get away with, the Russian leader supported the separatist insurgency with no endgame in mind except to further destabilize Ukraine. As Andrew S. Weiss put it, "Mr. Putin's efforts look more like a short-term tactical play than a carefully considered embrace of an ethnocentric approach to defending Russia's declared interests in the neighborhood"—and that was precisely what made the Ukraine showdown "even scarier and more dangerous."[3]

It is not impossible that Putin also saw the stealth invasion as an opportunity to perfect the hybrid warfare first applied in Crimea, a novel stratagem blurring the lines between soft and hard power, already praised by Western military professionals. A former NATO commander, Admiral James G. Stavridis, said he admired the "finesse" of the campaign in Crimea and that the strategy was applicable "no matter where you are operating in the world."[4]

The first important step was the decision to prompt Russian volunteers to organize through the Internet, set up recruiting sites and physical training camps and, last but not least, let them cross the Russo-Ukrainian border with weapons. Some of the most notorious volunteer commanders later claimed full responsibility for what happened next. "If my group had not crossed the border," one of them boasted, there would have been no real fighting: "Just a few dozen killed, burned, arrested. That would have been all."[5]

From the Ukrainian side, the "pro-government" forces also consisted largely of volunteers. The so-called volunteer battalions belonged to far-right groups and egomaniac millionaires. Azov Battalion, originating in the neo-Nazi movement, wore Waffen-SS symbols on its insignia. The billionaire Ihor Kolomoyski equipped the Dnipro Battalion.[6] And so on.

Radicals from Russia crossed into Donbass with ease. So did soldiers of fortune and sociopaths. Tim Whewell of the BBC described a grotesque mix of monarchists, secular nationalists, Orthodox mystics, and people who had signed up to "save the Russian state" from Western aggression. Aptly, Whewell reminded readers about the Russian tradition of volunteering abroad to protect Slavic "brethren": in Tolstoy's *Anna Karenina*, after the heroine dies, her lover Vronsky signs up to fight against the Turks in Serbia. In the 1990s, Russians fought alongside Serbs in the Yugoslav wars.

Other fighters were "clearly driven partly by an existentialist quest to give meaning to their lives," reading Albert Camus and Jean-Paul Sartre between battles. Because they all kept their mouths shut, it was impossible to tell whether a young man had joined the separatists "in search of money or adventure" or had been "ordered to Ukraine as part of an unofficial mission that will never be acknowledged," an article in the *New York Times Magazine* reported.[7]

After Putin decided to have boots on the ground, military professionals arrived, bringing advanced weapons such as Buk surface-to-air missiles. It is unlikely that the Russian high command planned attacks or calculated strategic costs in Donbass. Most probably, it just made sure that the separatists had everything necessary to sustain their armies. The Kremlin stayed in the shadows, allowing the leaders of the two "people's republics" every foolishness. The purpose was to keep the rebellion aflame.

At the end of 2014, *New York Times* correspondent Andrew Roth wrote: "The scale of destruction throughout the region is often breathtaking. Residential apartments bear craters from tank shells. Many places, especially smaller towns, lack basic utilities, like water and electricity. Power lines have been downed, mines flooded, substations incinerated and rail service halted." The "minister" of building, architecture, and utilities of the Luhansk "People's Republic," plucked straight "from the trenches," still sported a pistol on his hip. The regime imposed by the insurgents was a mixture of village justice, warlordism, and patriarchy. An attempt was made to prohibit single women from visiting bars and clubs.[8]

With Donbass, the Kremlin miscalculated. The annexation of Crimea had brought it only a slap on the wrist: Crimea *was* a disputed territory with a complicated past; the takeover had been bloodless. The insurgency in Donbass turned very bloody very early. The almost certainly accidental shooting down of a Malaysian plane in July 2014, by either separatists or the Russian military, epitomized the outrage felt around the world. The separatists obstructed the investigation while Moscow refused to acknowledge its presence in Donbass and blamed the Ukrainian air force. After that, sanctions against Russia began to hit at the very heart of the Russian economy—its energy sector and the banks sustaining it. Later in the year, Putin officially announced that Russia was in recession; he urged his compatriots to tighten their belts.[9] He wouldn't admit the presence of Russian military personnel in Donbass until December 2015.[10]

In the wake of the annexation of Crimea and war in Donbass,

Russia experienced an upsurge of jingoism and xenophobia, both spontaneous and Kremlin-propagated. The consequences are bound to be extensive: the unleashed aggression targets not just Ukraine or the West but virtually any group the Russian patriotic majority chooses to see as the Other—including domestic liberal opposition and every minority.

Referring to previous coups in the near abroad—in Georgia and Kirgizstan as well as Ukraine—Putin declared that the world could now see "what tragic consequences the wave of the so-called color revolutions has led to. . . . We have to do all that is needed to ensure that similar things never happen in Russia." His foreign minister seconded that: "The West is making clear it does not want to force Russia to change policy but wants to secure regime change."[11]

In December 2014, Russia officially adopted a new military strategy. The list of threats to Russia now included NATO "moving closer" to Russia's borders; political coups in neighboring countries and the installment of anti-Russian regimes there; and destabilization of Russia to promote "violent regime change."[12] The last accusation had not been heard from the Kremlin since the Stalin era.

By nurturing the insurgency in Donbass, Putin gambled with Russia's future in more ways than one. Unleashing the vengeful rabble was perhaps worse than losing standing with the great powers of the West. When, at some point, the Russian street turns its attention to corrupt administrators in Russia, the rioters are likely to use the same methods Russian volunteers used in Donbass: lynching, looting, killing. The tiger has tasted blood, and as Alexander Pushkin put it two centuries ago, God forbid one should ever witness a Russian rebellion, "senseless and merciless."[13]

Ukraine as a Failed State

By unleashing war in Donbass, Putin foolishly jeopardized the future of his regime, or "managed democracy" as his ideologues call it. But the other side in the conflict, Ukraine, simply collapsed as a state.

A state fails when it loses (in Max Weber's famous formulation) its monopoly on the legitimate use of physical force on its territory. The Ukrainian state has done that, and now also meets all the other criteria of a failed state: massive movement of refugees and domestically displaced persons, vengeance-seeking group grievance, the rise of factionalized elites, and the intervention of external actors.[14]

The movement of refugees and displaced persons is the largest in Europe since World War II; as of August 2015, according to United Nations data, at least 1.3 million people had been "internally displaced" within Ukraine, and 900,000 had fled abroad, mostly to Russia.[15]

"External actors"—Russia and NATO—were fighting a proxy war in Donbass. Vengeance-seeking groups enjoyed the support of about 5 percent of Ukrainian voters, but their influence was so disproportionately big that the failure of democracy in Ukraine was hard to dispute. David Stern of the BBC wrote that because no one in Kiev wanted to "provide fuel to the Russian propaganda machine," the presence of the far right in positions of authority went unmentioned. Meanwhile, according to Stern, commanders of the neo-Nazi Azov Battalion were close to the Ukrainian Ministry of Interior; one of them was named police chief of the Kiev region. After the Maidan uprising, the crime rate throughout Ukraine increased by 40 percent, military and police arsenals had been looted, and more weapons came from eastern Ukraine. In August 2015, members of another right-wing party, Oleh Tyahnybok's Svoboda, clashed with police in front of the parliament building in Kiev, killing three servicemen.[16]

Within a year, the power of warlords spread beyond the war zone. In July 2015, a Right Sector battalion clashed with government forces in the town of Mukachevo in western Ukraine. The fighting originated in a business dispute over trade in contraband cigarettes: Mukachevo sat on Ukraine's border with Hungary. Several people died; the weapons used included machine guns and grenade launchers.[17]

In 2015, more than forty private battalions existed in Ukraine. Besides Donetsk and Luhansk, several other areas were controlled by warlords. Among the most colorful was Ihor Kolomoysky, an oligarch commanding at least $3 billion, and a citizen of three countries—Ukraine, Cyprus, and Israel—who spent at least $10 million to create the Dnipro Battalion. He called Putin a "schizophrenic of short stature." Putin returned the compliment by calling him a "unique crook."[18]

The war in the east has been too bloody, too ugly, and too dishonest on both sides for any Ukrainian national unity to be feasible. Even after the bloodshed eventually ends, Ukraine will likely never be able to return to its 2013 borders.

Since the coup in February 2014, Ukraine has conducted two elections. In the first, held in May 2014, Petro Poroshenko won the presidency with 54.7 percent of the votes; the leader of the Orange Revolution of 2004, Yulia Tymoshenko, came in a distant second with 12.8 percent. In the October 2014 parliamentary election, six parties got into the new Rada, the winners being Prime Minister Arseniy Yatsenyuk's People's Front, with 22.1 percent of the vote, and President Poroshenko's party, somewhat tellingly called just Petro Poroshenko Bloc, with 21.8 percent. The Yatsenyuk-Poroshenko alliance began to crumble almost immediately. The government formed in November 2014 included three foreigners, one of whom could neither speak nor understand Ukrainian. The post of the minister of finance went to the American investment banker Natalie Jaresco, whose only qualifications for the job seemed to be Ukrainian roots and past employment with the U.S. Department of State. In May 2015, Poroshenko equally inexplicably appointed the former president of the Republic of Georgia, Mikheil Saakashvili, as the governor of Odessa Province.[19]

With each faction accusing others of corruption, the infighting mounted, resulting in ugly public brawls in the parliament and cabinet meetings. To Moscow's immense satisfaction, in February 2016 the Poroshenko-Yatsenyuk coalition collapsed.

All sides in the escalating power struggle appealed to the Ukrainian street, making another violent insurgency possible. Two years since Maidan, Ukraine had more factions and more fanaticism, and its prospects for nation-building were in decline. Putin's Kremlin couldn't be happier with the results.

Ukraine may be turning into another Yugoslavia, a young state that cannot survive except as a dictatorship. Both Ukraine and Yugoslavia belong to the category of artificial entities formed by foreign leaders: Yugoslavia at the Paris Peace Conference of 1919, Ukraine by Lenin in 1922. In both countries, people spoke a spectrum of dialects, the official language a sort of linguistic median. Both were also divided along religious and cultural lines. Iosip Broz Tito held Yugoslavia together; a viceroy appointed by Moscow did that for Ukraine. But absent its strongman and outside a Cold War context, Yugoslavia was not a coherent nation. Neither is Ukraine, and this is the ultimate cause of the present civil war.

Peace in Ukraine at the initial, promising stage of nation-building between 1991 and 2013 was made possible by the precarious balancing act of all four of its presidents, including the "pro-Western" Yushchenko and the "pro-Russian" Yanukovych. The February 2014 coup (call it a revolution if it makes you feel better) threw the country off balance, and the submerged interregional tensions surfaced with a boom.

A Russian Lake

On December 4, 2014, in his equivalent of the State of the Union address, Putin summed up the party line on Crimea. As befits a national fetish, the language he applied to the annexed territory was metaphysical. Referring to the semi-legendary baptism of Prince Vladimir in Chersonesus, he called Crimea the "spiritual foundation" of the Russian state. For Russia, Putin announced, Crimea had "an enormous civilizational and sacral meaning. Just like the Temple Mount in Jerusalem for those who practice Islam or Judaism."[20]

The allusion was new, idiosyncratic, and strange. For starters, clashes over the Temple Mount in Jerusalem have become an epitome of an unending conflict. Perhaps appropriately, the first federal investment in Crimean sacral grounds was an army group. Tanks and armored vehicles were ferried across the Kerch Strait with praiseworthy efficiency, up to fifty a day—an accomplishment given the sad state of the ferries.

In November 2014, the Russian Ministry of Defense confirmed that it had deployed a squadron of thirty jet fighters to Belbek air base. NATO's commander, General Philip Breedlove, in Kiev at the time, said that the ongoing Russian "militarization" of Crimea would have an effect on "almost the entire Black Sea."[21] In the 1950s–1960s, Taiwan was called the unsinkable U.S. aircraft carrier. Was Crimea about to become Russia's aircraft carrier?

The annexation of Crimea has changed the balance of power in the Black Sea. Under the terms of the United Nations Convention on the Law of the Sea of 1982, Russia now claims an exclusive economic zone along the peninsula's coastline—an avenue for underwater pipelines and a repository of fossil fuels. Ukraine, dispossessed, is losing its role as a transit corridor between Russia and Europe.

The Russian Black Sea Fleet had been stationed in Crimea before, as were some Russian air force units. With the annexation, the air force presence expanded; Russian ground troops, tanks, and armored personnel carriers arrived; the Russian military established a new army group on the peninsula. Russian ground troops now surround Ukraine from the north, east, and south. Just 450 miles separate the army groups in Crimea from those in Bryansk, across Ukraine's northern border. If they advanced simultaneously, the two could touch in central Ukraine within days. Along the Black Sea coast, the shipbuilding facilities of Ukrainian Mykolaiv are just 100 miles away from the Russian army group in Crimea; Odessa is 75 miles farther west; 25 miles more, and one is in Moldova.

With Russia having gained in the strategic balance, the influence of every other Black Sea nation, including Turkey, has shrunk. The United States and NATO have lost some of their clout in the eastern Mediterranean and the Middle East. To make this clear, in May 2015 Russia and China held their first joint naval exercises in the Mediterranean.

As the naval base at Sevastopol had been the focal point of the Russian Crimea myth and a major goal of the annexation rush, now the Black Sea Fleet found itself the center of attention. It also found a new role: intimidating every other Black Sea nation, as none is Russia's friend. Turkey, Bulgaria, and Romania are NATO members; Ukraine and Georgia have begged for membership. Another mission became Russian warships' regular visits to Syria, bringing arms to Moscow's friend Bashar al-Assad.

But contrary to the patriotic Russian myth, the Black Sea has never been a Russian lake, and despite the fears of Russia's neighbors, it will likely never be one. For two centuries, Russia has been the dominant naval power in the basin, but it is Turkey, not Russia, that determines the net balance. The Bosporus, the Sea of Marmara, and the Dardanelles, collectively known in European diplomacy as the Straits, belong to Turkey, and it is up to Turkey alone to determine who will have access to the Black Sea and on what conditions. All other Black Sea countries are in the situation of a homeowner whose driveway is separated from the turnpike by somebody else's property.

Globally, the Straits are not as important as the Suez and Panama canals, or Gibraltar. Those three serve every seafaring nation; the Straits serve only the Black Sea countries. Yet they are a lifeline for Bulgaria, Georgia, Romania, and Ukraine, their only oceanic connection. To that, add the landlocked nations of the Caucasus—Armenia and Azerbaijan—and also the five "stans" of post-Soviet Central Asia. Russia's Eurasian coastline is immense, but the Black Sea coast is the only one that is ice-free year round. Close the Straits, and Russian commerce will suffocate. Open the Straits to powers at war with Russia, and the Russian navy will bleed.

In the Crimean War, Turkey turned the Straits into a highway for the British and French navies. In World War I, it let its ally, Germany, send cruisers into the Black Sea, largely incapacitating the Russian fleet there. In World War II, Ankara refused to let Germans and Italians in, thus saving the Soviets from losing the south.[22]

The international treaty regulating the Straits—the Montreux Convention of 1936—allows Turkey to close them to all foreign warships in times of war or when threatened by aggression. It may refuse access to the merchant ships of nations with which it is at war. In peacetime, all civilian vessels are guaranteed free passage "by day and by night, under any flag with any kind of cargo." The transit of naval vessels is regulated, and the passage of naval ships not belonging to the Black Sea nations is heavily restricted. Outsiders' warships must be under 15,000 tons, the guns they carry under 203 millimeters. No one, including the Black Sea nations, may send an aircraft carrier through the Straits.

These provisions have been charged with conflict from the day the convention was signed. After 1945, wanting uninhibited access to the Mediterranean, Stalin demanded that Ankara cede him "joint ownership" of the Straits. That strategic pressure led U.S. president Harry Truman in 1947 to proclaim the Truman Doctrine, in which he pledged support of every nation threatened by the USSR, a move many historians consider to have launched the Cold War. Though universal in its wording, the Truman Doctrine was specifically crafted to protect Turkey and its Mediterranean neighbor Greece.

Grudgingly, the Soviets caved in. To evade the ban on aircraft carriers, they designated the only two they had—the *Kiev* and the *Admiral Kuznetsov*—as "aircraft carrying cruisers." They usually passed through the Bosporus at night; Orhan Pamuk writes in his Istanbul memoir: "A great hulk, growing larger and larger as it rose from the pitch-dark sea and approached the closest hill—the hill from which I was watching—this was a colossus, a leviathan, in shape and size a specter from my worst nightmares, a Soviet warship!—rising out of the night and the mist as if in a fairy tale, a vast floating fortress."[23]

NATO had to use semantic evasions as well. In the 1960s, when the United States started sending ships armed with 305-millimeter missiles into the Black Sea, the Soviet Union complained that this violated the 203-millimeter limit. NATO responded by saying that the Montreux Convention did not mention missiles, only guns. The superpowers' semantic dodging was a Cold War equivalent of the joke about the priest who, when reproached for eating a chicken on a Friday, christened it a fish.

With the annexation of Crimea, Russian share of control over the region spiked. The Ukrainian navy—or what was left of it—evacuated to Odessa. Another, indirect victim of the annexation was the Republic of Georgia. In 2008, Russia and Georgia fought a short war with lasting consequences. Georgia has strong NATO aspirations and had sided with Ukraine against Russia in the past. The Russian annexation moved Ukraine so far west that military cooperation between Tbilisi and Kiev is now all but impossible. For Russia, the acquisition of Crimea makes every hostile act against Georgia—intelligence collecting, sea traffic blockade, or military strikes—infinitely easier. If Russia ever lays siege to Ukrainian and Georgian ports, that may be the end of sovereignty for both. Russian strategists undoubtedly want as much control over the Black Sea as the United States holds over the Caribbean.

The worst-case strategic scenario for Russia on the Black Sea would be the closure of the Straits to Russian vessels, paired with foreign naval intervention—in other words, the repetition of the Crimean War and World War I. For that to happen, Turkey must be at war with Russia, a scenario hard to imagine only a year ago, but not totally unthinkable now, since the two powers clashed over Syria.

Also, Russia's adversaries do not even need Turkey's cooperation to block the Straits at their southern end, at the Dardanelles in the Mediterranean. Position a naval force in international waters there, and the hostile fleet will stop all the Russian traffic. This may turn out to be the way to impose the severest sanctions on the Russian economy.

Energy

If there is one achievement that Vladimir Putin can be truly proud of, it would be a series of carefully engineered victories in energy wars. Crimea is a monumental foothold in that battle.

According to the Convention on the Law of the Sea, coastal states "have sovereign rights" in a 200-nautical-mile "exclusive economic zone" where they own the natural resources on the sea floor. The annexation of Crimea has added 36,000 square miles to Russia's exclusive economic maritime zone in the basin, more than tripling its size.[24]

There are gas fields in the Black Sea and the Sea of Azov. Until recently, these reserves did not seem terribly important: the Ukrainian company that owned and developed the fields, Chernomorneftegaz, accounted for just 5 percent of Ukraine's energy production.

In the past few years, however, there have been reports suggesting large fossil fuel fields in the basin.

As in Marco Polo's time, today the Black Sea is again the terminus of a transcontinental route—this time not for silk but for gas. With the annexation, a new Russia-to-Europe gas pipeline bypassing Ukraine could be built mostly in Russian waters. There is an option of laying part of it through Crimea, or very close to its coast, cutting the costs of construction and operation.

When the European Union, to punish Russia, put the South Stream project on hold, Putin just scrapped the whole thing, flew to Turkey, and negotiated an alternative: an undersea pipeline taking Russian gas to the Turkish border with Greece. With a planned annual capacity of 63 billion cubic meters, the project was christened Turkish Stream.[25]

Putin's geopolitical rationale had been based on the premise that although Turkey is a NATO country, it is thoroughly un-Western, and in the previous decade progressively *anti*-Western. That is still true, but Turkey became Russia's enemy the moment Moscow intervened militarily in the Syrian conflict, and the Turkish Stream project stalled.

In the meantime, Gazprom agreed to buy out the Western companies that had signed up for the aborted South Stream—Italian Eni, German Wintershall, and Electricité de France. The contractor to build the South Stream was the Italian company Saipem, and until the spring of 2015, Gazprom paid Saipem the costs of keeping its two enormous pipe-laying vessels in the Black Sea, idling at the Bulgarian port of Varna.[26]

To keep its energy monopoly in the Black Sea area, Moscow strongly discourages every attempt at developing fracking in Ukraine and Romania. In December 2014, Chevron backed out of a deal with a government-owned Ukrainian company to develop gas fracking in western Ukraine, negotiated a year earlier.[27] NATO's secretary general at the time, Anders Fogh Rasmussen, believed that Moscow was underwriting Eastern European environmentalists' anti-fracking campaigns: "I have met allies who can report that Russia, as part of their sophisticated information and disinformation operations, engaged actively with so-called non-governmental organizations— environmental organizations working against shale gas—to maintain European dependence on imported Russian gas."[28]

EIGHT

#CrimeaIsOurs

After the annexation, the Russian middle class fell into a strange euphoria, turning a blind eye to the diplomatic, financial, and political costs of Putin's Crimean Reconquista. Flights to the peninsula were overbooked: people felt moved to support the region's economy. #CrimeaIsOurs became the hashtag of Russian social networks.

Basking in popularity, Putin interpreted the future of Crimea casually, giving simple answers to difficult questions. Russia had just developed Sochi, with its expensive hotels empty since the 2014 Winter Olympics; now it had to fill another resort in the face of the world's disapproval. Putin dismissed the problem, saying that Sochi would be for the "moneyed" and Crimea for the "ordinary people." Plans were made to open casinos, to turn Crimea into a Russian Las Vegas. But very quickly, Crimeans realized that the bright future promised by Moscow was far away, if it was to come at all.

Economy

The peninsula got 80 percent of its electricity and 85 percent of its water from Ukraine. Now Kiev retaliated. Power outages plunged Crimean towns into darkness. Ukraine shut down the North Crimea Canal, which supplied the peninsula with Dnieper River water, effectively killing large-scale agriculture in the region. Crimea had gotten nearly 90 percent of its imports by rail. The railroads, naturally, passed through Ukraine, and now shut down.[1]

The Kerch Straits crossing had been better served in Marco Polo's time. Ferries were few. Moscow either had not foreseen the closure of the land route to Crimea or decided travelers would put up with hardship. Regular closures of ferries because of inclement weather were a Kerch staple, but they had never been more than an inconvenience. Now, whenever a hurricane-force northeaster shut down traffic for five days in a row, it was a *problem*. Fistfights flared up; truck drivers mutinied, blocking the landing altogether.[2]

Crimeans found themselves on an island—shipwrecked.

On the eve of the annexation, in December 2013, out of 2.3 million Crimeans, only 251,000 were employed. Even those with jobs were, as I mentioned, the worst-paid workers in Europe. Technically, Crimea should have been considered a catastrophe, with each working person supporting eight dependents, and on the scantiest of wages. But things in the post-Soviet space are rarely what they seem. Since 1991, Crimea had grown a robust shadow economy serving 6 million tourists a year: rooms for rent, food stalls, guided tours, escorts, illicit substances, all bought with cash. At least 70 percent of hotels, hostels, and vacation rentals operated in the shadow economy. Obviously, none of their revenues reached the treasury in taxes. Kiev subsidized 52 percent of Crimea's budget.[3]

Putin had doubled Crimeans' pensions and state employees' salaries, but most workers nevertheless took a hit. First, small businesses were now taxed (registering all rentals had become mandatory), and although Russia was hardly a paragon of law-abidance and its taxation rate is among the lowest in the world, this was a loss for entrepreneurs spoiled by Kiev's lenience. Second, despite the patriotic fever in mainland Russia, in the summer of 2014 Crimea got barely half of its typical tourist flow: it was a conflict zone, its transportation link to the mainland had been severed, and so had its water and energy supplies. Three million tourists visited, versus 5.9 million in 2013. These numbers failed to improve during the 2015 season.[4]

There are only a handful of established businesses on the peninsula. Crimea's tourism sector had failed to develop into an industry, first because of the overcentralized management from Kiev and Moscow, then because of the chaos of the transition period with its gangster privatization and consequent random takeovers. Environmental degradation had undermined the fisheries; the famed Black Sea oysters became all but extinct, eaten by a stowaway Pacific mollusk that had arrived on ship bottoms in the 1950s, the Sea of Azov sturgeon overfished by poachers. Crimean agriculture still harvests the follies of central planning. Growing rice in Crimean steppes inherently prone to droughts proved ultimately unsustainable. A noxious profitable plant tobacco, when grown on Crimean plantations, is just noxious: apparently, its quality has not improved one tiny bit since the 1850s, when Leo Tolstoy complained about its disgusting taste in his Sevastopol diary.[5]

One of the few reputable enterprises is Massandra Winery, founded in 1894, some say at the behest of Tsar Nicholas II. The "reunification" made Massandra workers so happy that they painted a forklift with the colors of the Russian flag, but it did little for the winery's sales. Massandra wines are about as popular on world markets as Scottish haggis. They belong to the category of fortified wines—sherry, port, madeira, drinks whose heyday is long past and whose very limited connoisseur market is largely owned by Portugal and Spain. Energized by what they saw as new opportunities, the Massandra winemakers announced that their product was special because it was fortified with beetroot ethanol, not grape brandy like in Europe. But instead of getting showered with orders from London and New York, their sales in Russia plummeted: Russian epicures were horrified to discover that all those decades they had been drinking glorified moonshine. Within a year, Crimean wine sales were off by 61 percent.[6]

Crimean agriculture plummeted as well. Irrigation, credit, and exports became difficult, if not impossible to secure. The leader of the Crimea Farmers Association dryly commented: "On a scale of one to five, we are at negative three."[7]

Moscow recklessly sanctioned the reapportioning of property on the peninsula. According to a recent *New York Times* correspondent's estimate, more than $1 billion in "real estate and other assets have been stripped from their former owners," including "banks, hotels, shipyards, farms, gas stations." The victims of confiscation maintain that the Crimean government received "carte blanche" from Moscow to fund its budget by whatever means available. Calling the confiscations "nationalization," the authorities focused on property belonging to Ukrainians—both oligarchs and small businesses—but Russian-owned enterprises were not necessarily spared. "Nationalization" of that kind heralds a long period of seizure of the spoils of annexation, with economic growth the least of anyone's worries.[8]

Violating E.U. sanctions, on September 17, 2014, the Greek cruise liner *Ocean Majesty*, chartered by a German tourist agency, dropped anchor at Yalta. As the first European ship to visit the peninsula since the annexation, it caused a media splash. Only 330 of the 436 tourists on board dared to go ashore. But the visit did not augur a return to normalcy: in December 2014, the European Union imposed a ban on E.U. cruise ships visiting Crimean ports.[9]

The new set of sanctions was aimed not at Russia but at Crimea.

European businesses were prohibited from investing in or trading with the peninsula. Energy and telecommunications deals were specifically prohibited. In a coordinated move, a day later the White House also introduced sanctions against the peninsula. President Obama said the goal was "to provide clarity to U.S. corporations doing business in the region and reaffirm that the United States will not accept Russia's occupation and attempted annexation of Crimea." The U.S. Treasury Department placed new restrictions on Crimean companies and individuals supporting the separatist cause. Among the latter were members of the Night Wolves motorcycle group, who had been prominent during the takeover. Predictably, that had the Sevastopol bikers howling with joy about the free publicity and mockingly challenging the U.S. government to punish them more.[10]

The local and regional elections in Crimea and Sevastopol in September 2014 could not be dismissed as a sham. The results were real, and they demonstrated continuing support for Moscow and Putin. The turnout was 53.6 percent, which was very high: city elections held in Moscow the same day saw turnout of just 20.2 percent. Twelve parties had participated in the campaign, but only two won any seats. Out of 75 new members of the Crimean State Council, 70 represented Putin's United Russia party, and 5 were from the right-wing party known as LDPR. Again, the Crimea proved far more conservative than the capital, where United Russia won only 28 seats out of 45 and the LDPR 1.[11]

The majority of Crimean Tatars boycotted the vote.

Kirim

So far, Crimea has been spared the horrors of the civil war—by good luck rather than good management. Meanwhile, the socioeconomic plunge Crimea is taking promises social unrest. And then there is the Tatar "problem."

Because Tatars returned to Crimea in the 1990s as squatters, they are now required to "renegotiate" lease and property rights with the Russian government—a road to immense abuse and predictable injustice. The founders of the Crimean Tatar national movement plainly refuse to participate in the Russian state in any manner. In retaliation, Russian authorities have banned their leader, Mustafa Dzhemilev, from Crimea. They have also threatened to end the "dual power" on the peninsula if the Tatars' legislative bodies, the Qurultai and Mejlis, refuse to recognize the annexation. Meanwhile, Moscow promoted a loyalist Tatar movement, Kirim, led by Remzi Ilyasov, a former vice-chairman of Mejlis. With Crimean Tatars, Putin was attempting what Americans had been trying to achieve in Afghanistan and Iraq for over a decade: foster a friendly force.

Exiled to Kiev, Dzhemilev responded to Moscow's threats by saying that if they were carried out, he would take Tatar power structures underground. Until then, he pointed out, the struggle of the Tatars had been executed by peaceful means; now all options were on the table.[12]

Dzhemilev's Russian opponents do not appear to understand how incredibly lucky they are that he is the Crimean Tatar leader. For twenty years, he has been restraining the radicals within the movement. Nor do the Russians seem to acknowledge that an intercommunal conflict spreads like wildfire. It does not take many hotheads to turn a territory into a Beirut or a Sarajevo.

There is evidence that some Crimean Tatars have gone to Syria to join ISIS. As early as May 2014, a Crimean Tatar military commander in Syria, Andul Karim Krymsky [of Krym], addressed compatriots on the peninsula in a video, arguing that the West was not going to save them and advocating armed struggle against Russians instead. Yet when the pro-Russian mufti Ruslan Saitvaliev announced at a press conference that five hundred Crimean Tatars were already fighting for ISIS, that was most likely a gross exaggeration. Meanwhile, for the authorities, the ISIS specter became the pretext to arrest Tatar activists indiscriminately.[13]

In Crimea, ISIS is more or less an imagined influence. In Turkey, not so. Crimea used to be part of the Ottoman Empire, and Turkey is now a staunch supporter of Crimean Tatars. Under Recep Tayyip Erdogan's AKP (Justice and Development party), Turkey is redefining its cultural identity and regional role. Shunned by the European Union and feeling used by NATO, it is moving away from Europe. Crimea is part of its legacy, and some Tatar communities in Anatolia formed by nineteenth-century Crimean exiles are still in place.

The Russian annexation brought Crimea back on to Turkey's national agenda; in 2015–2016, Russian bombings of Syria, a country Turkey considers its backyard, made Turkish mainstream opinion firmly anti-Russian.

A rose is a rose under any other name, but a nation is not. To claim nationhood, the group has to shed its dual identity—"Crimean" *and* "Tatar"—and forge a single unambiguous face. "Crimean Tatar" implies the existence of a bigger Tatar nation, linking Crimean Tatars to the Tatars of Volga, Central Asia, and Siberia. Clearly, this reading undermines their claim on Crimea. It makes them another part of the peninsula's population, like Crimean Russians or Crimean Greeks.

As a centerpiece of their nation-building, Dzhemilev and his fellow leaders emphasize that "Crimean Tatars" are not a branch of the general Tatar population but a unique people, a merging of Mongol, Kipchak, Goth, Greek and other groups, the sum of the peninsula's history, not a mere particle of it.[14]

That this reading of history is a recent construct does not undermine its validity. The tricky (and dangerous) part is defining the endgame. Let's assume that the Kirim concept gets accepted by the

Tatars and their neighbors: the Kirim are the sum of every indigenous people of Crimea of the past two or three millennia. Where do they go from there? An independent Kirim state is not a realistic option. The majority of the Crimean Tatar diaspora remains in Central Asia, Turkey, and the Balkans, with no plans of ever resettling in Crimea. Even if the entire diaspora moved back (and such a move were economically sustainable), they would still be a minority in today's Crimea.

If Tatars ever develop a true national liberation movement, it will be a disaster for all involved. Crimea would turn into another Bosnia, except that instead of fighting a small, weak state like Serbia, the Crimean Tatars would be up against the much more powerful Russia.

Another dangerous scenario would be Ukraine trying to reclaim the peninsula by force. This would be a foolish move. Strategically, Crimea is an island, and thus difficult to seize; a Russian retaliatory strike would most likely take their troops to Nikolayev and Odessa; and the crisis could end with the whole Ukrainian Black Sea coast becoming another "people's republic" under Moscow's patronage. Nor is there much reason to believe that the majority of Crimeans would support reunification with Ukraine. Yet "restoration of Ukrainian sovereignty in Crimea" has found its way on the agenda of some powerful private foreign policy institutions in the United States, such as the Atlantic Council and Freedom House.[15]

In 1786, the British socialite and writer Elizabeth Craven reported: "The Crimea might with great ease be made an island." In 1979, the Soviet writer Vasily Aksyonov wrote a novel called *The Island of Crimea* that became an instant samizdat bestseller. It took a counterfactual approach to history, exploiting a real occurrence: during the Civil War, in 1920, Crimea became the last stronghold of the Whites. Had Britain, France, and the United States provided the support the White commanders begged for, Crimea could have seceded and become an alternative to the Soviet Union, a Russian Taiwan. In the novel, a twenty-two-year old British lieutenant, Richard Bayley-Land, aboard the dreadnaught *Liverpool* opens artillery fire on the Reds storming the Perekop, triggering a chain of events that leads to victory for the Whites. (Interviewed by the reporters, the sly, aristocratic, and hard-drinking Bayley-Land insists he did it "just for fun.")[16]

Aksyonov's novel articulated a historically Crimean trend: the peninsula's tendency to break away from bigger entities. The Crimean independence movement is not exactly around the corner, but it is in the making. There is, for example, a concept of Crimea as "testing grounds of a new common Eurasian culture." And the peninsula is becoming multicultural again. As early as the 1990s, minority groups included 2,794 Armenians; 2,166 Bulgarians, 3,000 Greeks, 17,000 Jews, 898 Karaims, 900 Krymchaks, and 3,000 Germans.[17]

The "reunification" with Russia has brought the people of Crimea nothing but grief. By 2016, power supplies from Ukraine had stopped completely, and blackouts became the new norm. Schools, hospitals, apartment buildings, cinemas, government offices—all got electricity and heating only sporadically. With streetlights off, driving turned hazardous. The most expensive restaurants in Yalta advertised as places where one could get warm (they had reserve generators, or so the ads claimed).

Destitution of such magnitude hadn't been seen on the peninsula since World War II. Wolves, extinct in Crimea in the twentieth century, returned (they had crossed the Sea of Azov on ice), and were spotted in towns foraging for food. As I am writing this, the City of Russian Glory, Sevastopol, is considering ordering pharmacies to start selling medications by the *pill*.

In two years since the annexation, the Kremlin had done nothing for the population. Only when the blackouts peaked at the end of 2015 did Moscow order the construction of the so-called "energy bridge"—simply put, an underwater cable bringing electricity to Crimea from the mainland across the Kerch Strait. Incidentally, no Russian company was ready to build at such short notice, and the Kremlin had to hire a Chinese contractor. A *real* bridge across the Kerch Strait, promised to Crimeans since day one of the annexation, is still in its prenatal stage.

All of this—sudden deprivation, Moscow's indifference, inept, corrupt local government—breed new political activism on the peninsula. It must be said that returning to Ukraine is not a realistic option—at least not until the Ukrainian state is strong enough to curtail the power of the right-wing paramilitary forces, which would be only too happy to descend on Crimea looking for violent revenge.

If (when?) Crimea finds itself in a position to secede, the position of the United States will be crucial. So will be the choices Americans will be forced to make.

NINE

You Break It, You Run

With at least nine thousand people killed and more than 2 million displaced, and with relations between Russia and the West set back by three decades, did we really, as many analysts suggest, sleepwalk into a new cold war? Or is the conflict just a seismic outburst, after which the relationship will go back to its chilly normal? With Europe in a state of disarray not seen since early in the postwar era, interpretations are difficult, and there is no agreement on the nature of the historical period we live in.

David Brooks of the *New York Times* finds the scope of the problems Americans face "way below historic averages. . . . Our global enemies are not exactly impressive. We have the Islamic State, a bunch of barbarians riding around in pickup trucks, and President Vladimir Putin of Russia, a lone thug sitting atop a failing regime." Pope Francis has repeatedly voiced an opposing assessment, calling our times a third world war "fought piecemeal, with crimes, massacres, destruction."[1]

Pacta Sunt Servanda

As an international law specialist, Yuval Shany, noted, the "combined effect of the international response to Crimea and Kosovo throws international law on self-determination into a state of uncertainty, threatening the stability of the existing state system."[2] The Crimean takeover has rendered five international accords meaningless, thereby deflating an important underlying principle of international cohabitation, *pacta sunt servanda*—that treaties should be honored.

The annulled agreements include the Belovezh Accords of December 8, 1991, which declared all fifteen republics of the former USSR sovereign and independent successor states; the Alma Ata Protocols of December 21, 1991, establishing the post-Soviet community of equals, the Commonwealth of Independent States, and mutually recognizing the member states' borders; the Partition Treaty on the Status and Conditions of the Black Sea Fleet of May 28, 1997, leasing Crimean military bases to Russia; and the Russian-Ukrainian "Naval Base for Gas" Accord, extending the Russian navy's lease in Sevastopol until 2042.

The final international agreement that was cast aside, and the one with the most lasting consequences, is the Budapest Memorandum of December 5, 1994, providing national security assurance to Ukraine after it surrendered its portion of the Soviet nuclear arsenal and joined the Non-Proliferation Treaty. Signed by the heads of state of Ukraine, Russia, the United States, and the United Kingdom, it called upon each of the latter three to "respect the independence and sovereignty and the existing borders of Ukraine" and to "refrain from the threat or use of force against the territorial integrity or political independence of Ukraine" or from "economic coercion."[3] Obviously, during the Crimea and Donbass crises, the United States and Britain failed to guarantee Ukraine's "existing borders." As a result, any other nuclear state in the world, if offered a similar arrangement, need not think twice before rejecting such a guarantee as worthless.

But what else could the United States and Britain do after Russia annexed Crimea, without risking direct military confrontation with Moscow? No one expected the guarantors of 1994 to do for Ukraine what Britain and France did for Poland in 1939 after Hitler invaded, and declare war on the aggressor. But the ambiguity of the security commitment to Ukraine raises serious questions about a bigger issue: Article 5 of the NATO Treaty, which in the popular understanding requires all members to come to the aid of any member subject to military attack. If Russia invades, for example, Estonia, in order to "rescue" its disgruntled Russian minority, many of whom hold Russian citizenship, what would NATO do?

If the Ukrainian crisis is any indication, the great powers of the West may be inclined to exercise caution. The underappreciated thing is that Article 5 actually lets them limit their response to the minimum they choose. Its spirit is "one for all, and all for one," but its letter is not. Formulated with enviable foresight, this is what it says:

> The Parties agree that an armed attack against one or more of them in Europe or North America shall be considered an attack against them all and consequently they agree that, if such an armed attack occurs, each of them, in exercise of the right of individual or collective self-defence recognised by Article 51 of the Charter of the United Nations, will assist the Party or Parties so attacked by taking forthwith, individually and in concert with the other Parties, such action as it deems necessary, including the use of armed force, to restore and maintain the security of the North Atlantic area.
>
> Any such armed attack and all measures taken as a result thereof shall immediately be reported to the Security Council.

Such measures shall be terminated when the Security Council has taken the measures necessary to restore and maintain international peace and security.[4]

The reference to the U.N. Security Council is not very practical, as Russia and its diplomatic partner China have veto powers there. What is practical, however, is the exact wording of the "one for all" principle: each NATO country will "assist" the party under attack by taking "such action as it deems necessary." Despite the expectations of Eastern European nations on Russia's border, soft economic sanctions against the aggressor would legally suffice. If you read the fine print of Article 5 closely, it's hard not to see that in promoting NATO expansion in the 1990s, and waking up Russia's aggressiveness in the process, Washington did not guarantee new NATO members' security even on paper.

One may question whether the eastward expansion has made the NATO alliance stronger. In a fleet on a combat mission, the slowest ship determines the speed of the entire force. Recent NATO members such as Estonia, Latvia, and Lithuania have nothing to contribute to the alliance militarily: they only add vulnerability. If there is a place where diversity does not belong, that would be a military alliance.

When the North Atlantic Treaty was signed in 1949, the founders included Belgium, Canada, Denmark, France, Iceland, Italy, Luxembourg, the Netherlands, Norway, Portugal, the United Kingdom, and the United States—a not entirely solid, but still acceptably united political core. Greece and Turkey, added in 1952, put the alliance on the USSR's southwestern flank, although these two did not really fit in with the group the way the other NATO countries did. The fact that the two went to war against each other over Cyprus in 1974 is sufficient proof of this. In the past decade, ideas for further NATO expansion have become grotesque: in

2007, Rudy Giuliani, then a presidential candidate, proposed adding Australia, India, Israel, Japan, and Singapore to the alliance.[5]

Every step forward in NATO expansion is paid for largely by the American taxpayer. Every member is supposed to devote 2 percent of its GDP to military spending, but as this is a recommendation, not a requirement, the vast majority of members find it easy to ignore. Only the United States, Britain, France, Greece, and Turkey meet the target, and the latter two are spending the money mainly to deter each other. If it is understandable that economically depressed Spain spends just 0.9 percent of its GDP on defense, Germany's 1.4 percent comes with no such excuse. President Barack Obama made his frustration clear at the September 2014 NATO summit in Wales; the meeting's final statement asked everyone to "move towards the 2% guideline"—but within a decade.[6]

The summit condemned Russia's "illegitimate occupation of Crimea and military intervention in eastern Ukraine" and ordered the creation of a "spearhead" force of several thousand troops prepared to deploy within a few days to respond to similar crises. Ten days later, 1,300 NATO troops from fifteen countries, including 200 Americans, began a military exercise called Rapid Trident around the Ukrainian city of Lviv. The Russian Foreign Ministry called that a continuation of NATO's eastward expansion and promised an "adequate" Russian response.[7]

On a broader scale, NATO's collective role remains problematic. The strategic response to the Crimean annexation has come mainly from the United States, whose Sixth Fleet, headquartered in Naples and traditionally focused on Libya, Egypt, and the Levant, has taken a renewed interest in the Black Sea. Typically nowadays, one U.S. warship is always on patrol in those waters. The NATO reconnaissance planes monitoring the area, shadowed and occasionally dangerously intercepted by Russian jets, are American too.[8]

NATO membership for Ukraine remains on the table. President Petro Poroshenko repeatedly voices his belief that "there is no other system in the world but NATO" that could ensure Ukraine's security. Although the prospect seems to arouse zero enthusiasm at NATO headquarters, it remains a faint possibility. The same applied to NATO membership for the Republic of Georgia, which by no stretch of imagination could be called a North Atlantic country.[9]

Rather dramatically, in December 2015, NATO invited another Eastern European nation to join the alliance: Montenegro. That was NATO's first expansion since 2009, and Russia angrily promised "retaliatory actions." Geopolitically, Montenegro is a burden. The country of 650,000 people has a military force of just 2,000, and its territory is hard to defend: the Adriatic Sea in the west provides an invader with several convenient gateways, and in the east Russia's friend Serbia waits.[10]

Despite the vast military power of the United States, there are many spaces on the globe where its presence simply cannot be introduced, even with casualties. The question is whether NATO has expanded to the edge of such a space, or past the edge.

How to Proceed?

The Crimea crisis has activated debates among competing schools in American foreign policy—neoconservatives, liberal interventionists, realists, isolationists, and paleoconservatives, to name just a few.

The harshest critique of America's handling of the crisis came from isolationists. Ron Paul called President Obama's sanctions against Russia "criminal" and declared that Crimea had a right to self-determination. Paul Craig Roberts angrily commented that on the hundredth anniversary of World War I, the Western powers were "again sleepwalking into destructive conflict," because "Washington interfering in the internal affairs of Ukraine" had led to developments beyond American control, raising the possibility of a "great power confrontation, which could be the end of all of us."

Oliver Stone announced that he would be making a documentary on the events in Kiev, dubbing what had happened "America's soft power technique called 'Regime Change 101.' . . . The West has maintained the dominant narrative of 'Russia in Crimea' whereas the true narrative is 'USA in Ukraine.' "[11]

Interventionists were largely pleased with the regime change in Kiev. The British historian Andrew Wilson called it an uprising "on behalf of everybody in the former Soviet Union," a delayed "anti-Soviet revolution" that, he hoped, might inspire copycat rebellions in other post-Soviet nations, Russia included. But for that to happen, interventionist intellectuals not unreasonably concluded, the White House had to intervene more aggressively. Michael McFaul, a "specialist in revolution" and the U.S. ambassador to Moscow for two years during the Obama administration, warned from his premature retirement that Putin's regime "must be isolated. The strategy of seeking to change Kremlin behavior through engagement, integration and rhetoric is over for now. . . . There must be sanctions, including against those people and entities— propagandists, state-owned enterprises, Kremlin-tied bankers— that act as instruments of Mr. Putin's coercive power. Conversely, individuals and companies not connected to the government must be supported, including those seeking to take assets out of Russia or emigrate."[12]

The leading neoconservative Robert Kagan saw the crisis as a test of America's ability to lead the world: "Many Americans and their political leaders in both parties, including President Obama, have either forgotten or rejected the assumptions that undergirded American foreign policy for the past seven decades. In particular, American foreign policy may be moving away from the sense of global responsibility that equated American interests with the interests of many others around the world and back toward the defense of narrower, more parochial national interests."[13]

Realists argued that interference in Ukraine—past, present, and proposed—did not further American interests but hurt them. This is what Henry Kissinger had to say: "Far too often the Ukrainian issue is posed as a showdown: whether Ukraine joins the East or the West. But if Ukraine is to survive and thrive, it must not be either side's outpost against the other—it should function as a bridge between them. . . . A wise U.S. policy toward Ukraine would seek a way for the two parts of the country to cooperate with each other. We should seek reconciliation, not the domination of a faction." Ambassador Jack F. Matlock: "Americans, heritors of the Monroe Doctrine, should have understood that Russia would be hypersensitive to foreign-dominated military alliances approaching or touching its borders."[14]

Strategy experts Dimitri Simes and Paul Saunders wrote in the *Washington Times* that if, in the fall of 2013, the White House and the European Union had "offered half of what they are now providing Ukraine, ousted President Viktor Yanukovych would likely have signed the E.U. deal that he abandoned instead. If the White House and Brussels had been willing to enforce the February 21 agreement, Ukraine would have had a new government without providing the Kremlin a pretext to seize Crimea or leverage for new demands. By trying to have it all in Ukraine for free, Mr. Obama blundered into disaster."[15]

Veterans of American politics George P. Shultz and Sam Nunn: "Recent history has shown the damage done to global security and the economic commons by cross-border threats and the uncertainty that emanates from them. As far as Russia is concerned, the world is best served when Russia proceeds as a respected and important player on the world stage. . . . A key to ending the Cold War was the Reagan administration's rejection of the concept of linkage, which said that bad behavior by Moscow in one sphere had to lead to a freeze of cooperation in all spheres. . . . Although current circumstances make it difficult, we should not lose sight of areas of common interest where cooperation remains crucial." Shultz and Nunn mentioned securing nuclear materials, destroying Syrian chemical stockpiles, and preventing nuclear proliferation on their list of such areas.[16]

One could add other items. If the United States is to continue the global "war on terror," cooperation with Russia is imperative, whether in intelligence gathering, covert operations, or the United Nations. The Northern Distribution Network, the elaborate web of land routes connecting American troops in Afghanistan to seaports in the Baltic and Pacific, runs through Russia. U.S. astronauts need Russian rockets to be able to travel to the International Space Station (in May 2014, reacting to U.S. sanctions, Russia announced that it was not interested in maintaining the ISS past 2020). Many American businesses have deep connections to partners in Russia. To name just two examples, ExxonMobil is drilling for oil in Siberia and the Arctic; and a company developing spaceships for NASA, Orbital Sciences Corporation, has been purchasing rocket engines from the Russian manufacturer Kuznetsov in Samara.[17]

The situation is paradoxical. In February 2016, the White House announced plans to quadruple military spending in Eastern European NATO countries. U.S. marines began prepositioning tanks and artillery in "classified" caves along the Norwegian-Russian border. Yet, at the same time, Washington started negotiating with Russia on the future of Syria and a joint fight against ISIS.[18]

If American rapprochement with Putin is still tentative and reversible, a number of European NATO countries want a solid anti-ISIS alliance with Moscow. In the immediate aftermath of the Paris terrorist attacks in November 2015, the French president François Hollande rushed to Moscow for consultations, breaking the diplomatic boycott of the Kremlin.[19]

Europe

If you listen only to American interventionists, you can get the impression that the single obstacle to European unity is Vladimir Putin. Unfortunately, things are not that simple. The main obstacle to European unity is Europe. The European Union, built and sold as a tightly knit alliance, was never meant to replace nation-states.

In the course of the crisis, "Europe" for all intents and purposes fell apart. Those of Russia's neighbors that were once part of the Russian empire—Poland, Estonia, Latvia, and Lithuania—demanded a strong response. Russia's economic partners—Germany, Italy, and France—tried doing business as usual.

Twenty-four hours after the infamous Crimea referendum, the Italian energy company Saipem pledged to build the offshore section of the South Stream gas pipeline. The state-of-the-art pipe-laying ship assigned to the task, *Saipem 7000*, was already a familiar sight on the Black Sea: Saipem had worked for Putin before, laying the Blue Stream pipeline that brought Russian gas to Turkey.[20]

On March 17, 2014, still at the peak of the Crimea crisis, E.U. energy commissioner Günther Oettinger said sanctions against Russia should not target the Russian economy. "It would be wrong," Oettinger said, "to question the economic ties that have been built over decades. They are important for the economy and jobs in Europe and Russia." Former chancellor Gerhard Schroeder went farther. At a meeting in St. Petersburg he proclaimed: "One should be speaking less about sanctions right now but instead about Russia's security interests." A furious John McCain declared that the leaders of Germany, starting with Angela Merkel, were "governed by the industrial complex." The comment caused outrage in Berlin, which deemed the senator's analysis "vicious nonsense."[21]

All of the big transnational oil companies, or "supermajors," do business with Russia—BP, Chevron, ExxonMobil, Royal Dutch

Shell, and Total, and three of the five are European. After a new set of sanctions was imposed in July 2014, BP lost $4.4 billion in market value within twenty-four hours. Austrian chancellor Werner Faymann commented: "I cannot approve of the euphoria of many in the EU over the success of sanctions against Russia. I see absolutely no cause for celebration. I do not know why we should be pleased if the Russian economy collapses."[22]

With Western sanctions still in place, in September 2015, European energy companies signed three major deals with Gazprom. These included an asset swap, joint development of Siberian oil and gas fields, and building a second Nord Stream pipeline under the Baltic Sea. This last agreement was equivalent to a geopolitical statement, as the pipeline would let Russia send more gas straight to Germany, bypassing Ukraine.[23]

In fairness to the Europeans, natural gas is a vital necessity, something that a nation might want to procure at all costs. But European trade with Russia is by no means limited to energy. At the time of the annexation, France was building two Mistral-class warships for Russia. Mistral is the amphibious assault ship that can carry up to sixteen helicopters, seventy tanks, and four landing barges. It is a perfect instrument of maritime aggression. When they signed the contract in 2011, the Russians had already decided on the names: one *Vladivostok*, another *Sevastopol*.

In 2014–2015, the deal became an embarrassment. The Russians had prepaid $900 million of the contract price of $1.3 billion. The Mistrals were being built at a shipyard in Saint Nazaire, at the mouth of the Loire. The local unions insisted that the town needed the seven thousand jobs the Russian order had secured. A union representative expressed hope that the deal would be the "start of a sustainable cooperation with Russia." The ships he said, were simply "big ferries" with a "few weapons."[24]

Several Eastern European E.U. members, such as Hungary and

the Czech Republic, objected to being dragged into a confrontation with Russia for strategic, economic, and status reasons. First, Russia was important economically; second, Hungary and the Czech Republic did not want the European Union to become a capitalist version of the Soviet-era COMECON, in which they, as junior partners, had to take orders from the headquarters; third, for Eastern Europe, Ukraine was a periphery, not necessarily deserving sovereignty, much less Western protection. In May 2014, the Hungarian government demanded from Kiev autonomy for the Hungarian minority in Ukraine—envisaging, one may assume, a little Hungarian Crimea. Hungarian prime minister Viktor Orbán is a vocal supporter of 3 million ethnic Hungarians in neighboring countries, whose ancestors ended up there after the Trianon Treaty of 1920. In 2014, Orbán started talking about "illiberal democracy," praising the example of Russia, China, India, and Turkey. After Senator McCain called him a "neo-fascist dictator getting in bed with Vladimir Putin," Orbán responded that he "would not be a viceroy in Hungary commissioned by some foreign state." The president of the Czech Republic, Miloš Zeman, called the U.S.-sponsored Kosovo an illegitimate state and said he wished the Czech Republic could take back its recognition. He defined the events in Ukraine as a civil war (a term most other E.U. countries refuse to use) and said Ukraine should become neutral.[25]

In Ukraine, the European Union had followed the principle, "You break it, you run": having disrupted Ukrainian politics with vain promises of a "European future," after the first shots were fired in Kiev the E.U. all but disappeared, leaving it to the United States to clean up the mess. It took the Europeans a year to return—but not as the European Union. Two great powers—Germany and France—began the process of mediation, their leaders conferring with the Ukrainian and Russian presidents on neutral territory, in authoritarian Minsk.

With the European Union undermined by the migrants crisis, and Russia seen as a strong ally in the fight against ISIS, European leaders are now likely to relegate war in Ukraine and annexation of Crimea to the icebox of diplomacy.

Intervention in the east was unpopular with Europeans from the start. The French philosopher Bernard-Henri Lévy complained in the *New York Times:* "To see the European Union acting so pusillanimously is very discouraging. France wants to hold on to its arms contracts for the jobs they are supposed to save in its naval shipyards. Germany, a hub of operations for the Russian energy giant Gazprom, is petrified of losing its own strategic position. Britain, for its part, despite recent statements by Prime Minister David Cameron, may still not be ready to forgo the colossal flows of Russian oligarchs' ill-gotten cash upon which the City, London's financial district, has come to rely."[26]

Some members of the American establishment tried to save Europe from itself. In May 2014, three U.S. congressmen, Eliot Engel, William Keating, and Michael Turner, sent a letter to NATO secretary general Anders Fogh Rasmussen, suggesting that NATO purchase or lease the Mistral warships being built for Russia. Five months later, Engel, Keating, and Turner, this time joined by four other members of Congress—Mike Rogers, Steve Chabot, Steve Cohen, and Gerry Connolly—repeated the idea in a letter to the new NATO chief, Jens Stoltenberg.[27]

But the French had decided to build the ships for Putin after Russia had already started a Reconquista by sending troops into Abkhazia and South Ossetia during the Russo-Georgian War in 2008. At that point, Putin's aggression in the near abroad did not seem unacceptable to Paris. *That* should have been seen as a real challenge to U.S. diplomacy, not the financial loss France faced in 2014.

Quite tellingly, when after unrelenting pressure from Washington the French government eventually cancelled the deal, it immediately sold the ships to another problematic customer—Egypt, with very little regard for what the two powerful assault carriers would do to the naval balance in the Middle East.[28]

In a recent book, noted international relations specialists Rajan Menon and Eugene Rumer warn that with the crisis in Ukraine the "consensus underpinning a European security order" has been torn apart, and that the "task facing Europe's leaders now is nothing less than fashioning a new European political and military order."[29]

A General and a Seagull

It is in our cultural code to choose David over Goliath, and a weaker nation challenging a stronger nation tends to attract our sympathy—as long as David and Goliath are not wrestling in our backyard, because, with humans, avoiding damage to self and property goes deeper than empathy.

Not just Davids but Goliaths too have interests, and we can't ignore them on moral grounds. A founding editor of *The American Conservative*, Scott McConnell, wrote that after the collapse of the USSR the West could choose between two models—that of 1815, when the defeated France was brought into the Concert of Europe, and that of 1919, when Germany was ostracized under the Versailles Treaty. George H. W. Bush, continued McConnell, clearly thought along 1815 lines, but his approach was incrementally "reversed by his successors, first by the Clinton-Albright duo, and then by his son, and now by Obama, the latter prodded by his belligerent assistant secretary of state Victoria Nuland."[30]

One can't help noticing that throughout the 1990s the policy makers of the West generally ignored Russia's national feelings. "Eat your spinach," representatives of the West said to the confused, angry nation, expecting it to emerge a smiling happy democracy. A great testimony in this respect comes from Jeffrey Sachs, the American economist advising Russians on "shock therapy" economic reform in the early 1990s. For Sachs, the crisis in Ukraine proved the road to Damascus, and this is what he had to say about it: "It took me 20 years to gain a proper understanding of what had happened after 1991. Why had the US, which had behaved with such wisdom and foresight in Poland, acted with such cruel neglect in the case of Russia? Step by step, and memoir by memoir, the true story came to light. The West had helped Poland financially and diplomatically because Poland would become the Eastern ramparts of an expanding NATO. Poland was the West, and was therefore worthy of help. Russia, by contrast, was viewed by US leaders roughly the same way that Lloyd George and Clemenceau had viewed Germany at Versailles—as a defeated enemy worthy to be crushed, not helped."[31]

Critique of Western universalism is among the underappreciated theses of Huntington's magisterial *Clash of Civilizations.* There is something in his interpretation of the West that can make liberals and conservatives equally uncomfortable: humility. Modernization, Huntington reminds us, "is distinct from Westernization and is producing neither a universal civilization in any meaningful sense nor the Westernization of non-Western societies." Consequently, efforts "to shift societies from one civilization to another are unsuccessful." Therefore, he concludes, the survival of the West depends on "Westerners accepting their civilization as unique not universal."[32]

By siding with "pro-Western" dissidents abroad, we compromise our values in the eyes of those peoples, undermine the future of the values we want to spread, and exacerbate divisions within the torn societies. In short, by interfering, we make an un-Western country anti-Western.

A popular point of view is that there used to be a "good" Russia, which later got corrupted into something evil. But it is incorrect to separate Vladimir Putin from the Russian Main Street. Within two decades, in the course of several acceptably free elections, the Russian majority has moved from laissez-faire democracy to soft authoritarianism. As Henry Kissinger succinctly put it, "For the West, the demonization of Vladimir Putin is not a policy; it is an alibi for the absence of one."[33]

As I write these words, Putin's approval rating in Russia stands at 86 percent. By the time you read them, it may have slipped to 60 percent or less. Russia may even have a new leader. But Putin's triumph or fall is not the point. The point is that it is precisely Russia's un-Westernness that makes the majority of Russians so proud.

The ideological disconnect between Russia and the West is strong again. This time, Russian elites and the majority of Russian voters swear not by Communism, but by civilizational particularism. They see the Russian civilization as distinctly separate from the rest of the world, including a specifically "native" understanding of people's rights and freedoms.

Desperate to see light at the end of the tunnel, a number of American analysts are now saying that there will be a "better" Russia after Putin. There might be. Or not. Most likely, there will be one, but only briefly. Russia will open up to the West for a decade or so, and then close down again, following its own endemic rhythm.

That should give us pause: Russia refuses to change, we refuse to accept that. But then again, as Antoine de Saint-Exupéry's king put it, "If I commanded a general to fly from one flower to the next like a butterfly, or to write a tragedy, or to turn into a seagull, and if the general did not carry out my command, which of us would be in the wrong, the general or me?"[34]

In the summer of 2014, President Obama, exasperated by critics asking for a clear sense of direction in and a philosophy of foreign policy, told reporters that his guiding principle in foreign affairs was

"Don't do stupid stuff" (according to witnesses, the president used a stronger word). His enemies immediately called that fecklessness and a comedown. His former secretary of state Hillary Clinton scolded the president in an interview with *The Atlantic*, pronouncing, "Great nations need organizing principles, and 'Don't do stupid stuff' is not an organizing principle."[35]

For sure, "First, do no harm" is not a principle that sits well with the twenty-first-century American zeitgeist. Don't just stand there, do something—we are being taught. Operate immediately, spike up the meds, be aggressive in treatment, can't you see that we are losing him/her (Libya/Ukraine)? Yet Obama's philosophy of non-maleficence did get endorsed by a number of renowned experts. David Remnick of *The New Yorker* approvingly commented: "When your aim is to conduct a responsive and responsible foreign policy, the avoidance of stupid things is often the avoidance of bloodshed and unforeseen strife. History suggests that it is not a mantra to be derided or dismissed."[36]

Future historians of the American presidency will, no doubt, uncover the reasons for and the ways in which Obama's principle of non-maleficence got hijacked in 2011–2014, but no matter their origins, the consequences of the follies in countries like Libya or Ukraine will be now felt for generations.

"Organizing principle" is an attractive expression, and when applied to foreign policy makes it sound as if the chaos of international relations could be scientifically controlled, like nuclear synthesis or tomato growing. It seems that for the interventionist the method is never to visit a developing country empty-handed, that is without non-negotiable gifts—business models, progressive mores, societal structures, political institutions, or "freedom" and "justice."

In the course of *The Atlantic* interview, Clinton blamed Obama for the emergence of ISIS, quoting his "failure" to help Syrian anti-Assad rebels as resolutely as she had helped the anti-Gaddafi rebels in Libya in 2011. But her critics may point out that it was the interventionist policy of blanket endorsement of the "Arab Spring," culminating in the NATO bombing of Libya, that made ISIS possible.

Taking out dictatorial regimes in North Africa and the Middle East created a structural void, where warlordism and lawlessness thrived. Libya is now a failed state in a key geopolitical location, and it is unclear whether the damage done to the nation is even repairable. Civil war rages, jihadism soars, and on the Libyan coast swarms of migrants fight for a place on a boat to cross the sea to Europe, the continent stupefied by the hundreds of thousands of refugees who have already arrived.

Compared with the brazen use of force in Libya, U.S. interference in Ukraine in 2013–2014 had been "soft." Yet its underlying principle was the same—impose a gift of "freedom" on a divided nation, and take it from there—again, in the spirit of the infamous Napoleonic motto *On s'engage, et puis on voit.*

"Do no harm" and "organize": the balance between the two in U.S. foreign policy will determine the fate of the unsettled parts of Eastern Europe, but also America's gains and losses on that gigantic isthmus stretching between the Baltic and the Black seas.

Notes

INTRODUCTION
Green Isle, Paradise Lost

1. Ebenezer Henderson, *Biblical Researches and Travels in Russia; Including a Tour in the Crimea and the Passage of the Caucasus* (London: James Nisbet, 1826), 291.
2. Charles King, *The Black Sea: A History* (New York: Oxford University Press, 2004), 12.
3. Neal Ascherson, *Black Sea* (New York: Hill and Wang, 1996), 5.
4. V. Badesku, "Release of Hydrogen Sulfide by Asteroid Impacts in Black Sea and Risks for Inland Human Population," *NCBI*, October 2007, www.ncbi .nlm.nih.gov/pubmed/17696133 (retrieved March 5, 2015).
5. H. D. Seymour, *Russia on the Black Sea and Sea of Azof* (London: John Murray, 1855), 294; Henry James, *The Turn of the Screw and Other Stories* (Köln: Könemann, 1996), 122.
6. "Crimea Profile—Overview," BBC, March 13, 2015, www.bbc.com/news/ world-europe-18287223 (retrieved August 11, 2015).
7. Harry de Windt, *Russia as I Know It* (Philadelphia: J. B. Lippincott, 1917), 184.
8. Ascherson, *Black Sea*, 9–10.
9. Erich Manstein, *Lost Victories* (St. Paul, Minn.: Zenith, 2004), 247.
10. Genesis, 2:11, in *Holy Bible: New Living Translation* (Wheaton, Ill.: Tyndale, 1996), 13.
11. Samuel P. Huntington, *The Clash of Civilizations and the Remaking of World*

Order (New York: Simon & Schuster, 2003), 193; Francis Fukuyama, *The End of History and the Last Man* (New York: Free Press, 2006).

12. Robert Kagan, "Superpowers Don't Get to Retire," *The New Republic*, May 26, 2014; "How to Spot a Russian Bomber," BBC, February 20, 2015, www.bbc .com/news/blogs-magazine-monitor-31537705 (retrieved February 20, 2015).

13. William Green Miller, "Foreword," in *Crimea: Dynamics, Challenges, and Prospects*, ed. Maria Drohobycky (London: Rowman & Littlefield, 1995), xiii.

ONE

Tower of Babel

1. "Ukraine: UK and EU Badly Misread Russia," BBC, February 20, 2015, www.bbc.com/news/uk-31545744 (retrieved February 20, 2015).

2. *The Book of Lech Walesa* (New York: Simon and Schuster, 1982), 144.

3. Robert Lansing, *The Peace Negotiations: A Personal Narrative* (Boston: Houghton Mifflin, 1921), 99–100; Tasker Bliss quoted in Margaret Mac-Millan, *Paris 1919: Six Months That Changed the World* (New York: Random House, 2001), 58.

4. Kagan, "Superpowers Don't Get to Retire."

5. Henry Kissinger, "To Settle the Ukraine Crisis, Start in the End," *Washington Post*, March 5, 2014.

6. Andrew C. Kuchins and Igor A. Zevelev, "Russian Foreign Policy: Continuity in Change," *Washington Quarterly*, Winter 2012, 151; Nicholas V. Riasanovsky and Mark D. Steinberg, *A History of Russia* (New York: Oxford University Press, 2011), 672.

7. Jack F. Matlock, *Reagan and Gorbachev: How the Cold War Ended* (New York: Random House, 2004), 318–319.

8. Elihu Root, "The Real Monroe Doctrine," *Proceedings of the American Society of International Law at Its Annual Meeting* (1907–1917), vol. 8, 428.

9. MacMillan, *Paris 1919*, 9; Root, "The Real Monroe Doctrine," 427.

10. Strobe Talbott, *The Russia Hand: A Memoir of Presidential Diplomacy* (New York: Random House, 2003), 80; Kissinger, "To Settle the Ukraine Crisis."

11. Richard Sakwa, *Frontline Ukraine: Crisis in the Borderlands* (London: I. B. Tauris, 2015), ix–x.

12. Giulio Andreotti quoted in Pavel Palazchenko, *My Years with Gorbachev and Shevardnadze: The Memoir of a Soviet Interpreter* (University Park: Pennsylvania State University Press, 1997), 158–159; James A. Baker III, *"Work Hard, Study . . . And Keep Out of Politics!": Adventures and Lessons from an Unexpected Public Life* (New York: G. P. Putnam's Sons, 2006), 291.

13. Bill Bradley, "A Diplomatic Mystery," *Foreign Policy*, August 22, 2009; Talbott, *The Russia Hand*, 441; Jack F. Matlock, "NATO Expansion: Was There a

Promise?" JackMatlock.com, April 3, 2014, http://jackmatlock.com/2014/04/
nato-expansion-was-there-a-promise (retrieved August 13, 2015).

14. Kohl quoted in Talbott, *The Russia Hand*, 226–227.

15. Madeleine Albright, "Enlarging NATO: Why Bigger Is Better," *The Econo-mist*, February 14, 1997.

16. Talbott, *The Russia Hand*, 225.

17. Ibid., 97–98, 225.

18. George F. Kennan, "A Fateful Error," *New York Times*, February 5, 1997.

19. Thomas L. Friedman, "Foreign Affairs; Now a Word from X," *New York Times*, May 2, 1998.

20. Huntington, *The Clash of Civilizations*, 158, 161.

21. Timothy J. Colton, *Yeltsin: A Life* (New York: Basic, 2008), 264–269.

22. Friedman, "Foreign Affairs; Now a Word from X."

23. Misha Glenny, *The Balkans: Nationalism, War, and the Great Powers, 1804–2011* (New York: Penguin, 2012), 652–662.

24. Talbott, *The Russia Hand*, 301.

25. Geoffrey Wheatcroft, "Who Needs NATO?" *New York Times*, June 15, 2011.

26. Glenny, *The Balkans*, 670.

27. Timothy Garton Ash, "The Kosovo Precedent," *Los Angeles Times*, February 21, 2008.

28. "Russia Resurgent," *The Economist*, August 14, 2008.

29. Wheatcroft, "Who Needs NATO?"

30. Mark R. Beissinger, "Promoting Democracy: Is Exporting Revolution a Constructive Strategy?" *Dissent*, vol. 53, no. 1, Winter 2006, 18–19.

31. Beissinger, "Promoting Democracy," 23.

32. "A Plea for Caution from Russia: What Putin Has to Say to Americans About Syria," *New York Times*, September 11, 2013; Kagan, "Superpowers Don't Get to Retire."

33. "A Plea for Caution from Russia: What Putin Has to Say to Americans About Syria"; Kagan, "Superpowers Don't Get to Retire."

34. "Senator John McCain: Russians Deserve Better than Putin," Pravda.ru, September 19, 2013, http://english.pravda.ru/opinion/19-09-2013/125705 -McCain_for_pravda_ru-0 (retrieved February 20, 2015).

35. "A Spotlight on Mr. Putin's Russia," *New York Times*, February 6, 2014.

36. Talbott, *The Russia Hand*, 76.

TWO

Protagonists

1. Ronald Suny, *The Soviet Experiment: Russia, the USSR, and the Successor States* (New York: Oxford University Press, 2011), 4.

2. "The Tale of Bygone Years" quoted in *Medieval Russia's Epics, Chronicles, and Tales,* ed. Serge A. Zenkovsky (New York: Meridian, 1974), 65–71.

3. Orest Subtelny, *Ukraine: A History* (Toronto: University of Toronto Press, 2000), 38; "The Battle on the River Kalka" quoted in *Medieval Russia's Epics,* ed. Zenkovsky, 193.

4. Subtelny, *Ukraine,* 70.

5. Ibid., 3, 23.

6. Samoil Velichko, *Letopis' sobytii v yugo-zapadnoi Rossii v XVII-m veke* (Kiev: Vremennaya komissiya dlya razbora drevnikh aktov, 1848), 44–45; Subtelny, *Ukraine,* 105, 133.

7. Y. V. Mann, *"Skvoz' vidnyi miru smekh . . . ": Zhizn N. V. Gogolya, 1809–1835 gg.* (Moscow: MIROS, 1994), 23–26; Subtelny, *Ukraine,* 231.

8. Paul Bushkovitch, *A Concise History of Russia* (New York: Cambridge University Press, 2012), 122.

9. Subtelny, *Ukraine,* 231.

10. Ibid., 307.

11. Benedict Anderson, *Imagined Communities: Reflections on the Origin and Spread of Nationalism* (London: Verso, 2006), 4; Serhiy Bilenky, *Romantic Nationalism in Eastern Europe: Russian, Polish, and Ukrainian Political Imaginations* (Stanford, Calif.: Stanford University Press, 2012), 7; Bushkovitch, *Concise History of Russia,* 326; Serhii Plokhy, *The Cossack Myth: History and Nationhood in the Age of Empires* (Cambridge: Cambridge University Press, 2012), 5; Taras Shevchenko, "Katerina," "Tarasova noch," ("Taras's Night"), "Ivan Pidkova" in *Kobzar* (Kyiv: Dnipro, 1985), 29, 44, 61–62; Mykhailo Hrushevsky, *History of Ukraine-Rus'* (Edmonton: Canadian Institute of Ukrainian Studies Press, 1997–2014).

12. *Letopis' samovidtsa* (Kiev: Kievskaya vremennaya kommissiya dlya razbora drevnikh aktov, 1878), 95; Lesya Ukrainka, "Negoda" ("Storm") in *Na krylakh pisen* (Lviv, 1893), 58–59. For detailed discussion of "mental maps" of Ukraine, see Bilenky, *Romantic Nationalism in Eastern Europe,* 71–100.

13. Subtelny, *Ukraine,* 359; Mikhail Bulgakov, *The White Guard* (New Haven: Yale University Press, 2008); J. A. E. Curtis, *Manuscripts Don't Burn: Mikhail Bulgakov, a Life in Letters and Diaries* (Woodstock, N.Y.: Overlook, 1992), 6.

14. MacMillan, *Paris 1919,* 71; Subtelny, *Ukraine,* 371.

15. Robert Service, *Lenin: A Biography* (Cambridge, Mass.: The Belknap Press, 2000), 455, 468–469; Suny, *The Soviet Experiment,* 308.

16. Subtelny, *Ukraine,* 499.

17. Bilenky, *Romantic Nationalism in Eastern Europe,* 303; Suny, *The Soviet Experiment,* 435; Subtelny, *Ukraine,* 500.

18. Jack F. Matlock, *Autopsy of an Empire: The American Ambassador's Account of the Collapse of the Soviet Union* (New York: Random House, 1995), 700.

19. Huntington, *The Clash of Civilizations,* 137, 139, 165.

20. Colton, *Yeltsin*, 206.

21. Duygu Bazoglu Sezer, "Balance of Power in the Black Sea in the Post-Cold War Era: Russia, Turkey, and Ukraine," in *Crimea: Dynamics, Challenges, and Prospects*, ed. Maria Drohobycky (London: Rowman & Littlefield, 1995), 167.

22. Sezer, "Balance of Power in the Black Sea," 179; *The Black Sea Pilot* (London: Hydrographic Office, Admiralty, 1884), 101. An American pilot repeats the warning almost verbatim: *The Black Sea Pilot* (Washington: Hydrographic Office, U.S. Navy, 1920), 279.

23. Roman Solchanyk, "Crimea: Between Ukraine and Russia," in *Crimea*, ed. Drohobycky, 7.

24. Angus Roxburgh, *The Strongman: Vladimir Putin and the Struggle for Russia* (New York: I.B. Tauris, 2013), 259.

25. Marshall I. Goldman, *Petrostate: Putin, Power, and the New Russia* (New York: Oxford University Press, 2010), 154.

26. Quoted in Talbott, *The Russia Hand*, 354.

27. Daniel Yergin, *The Prize: The Epic Quest for Oil, Money, and Power* (New York: Free Press, 2009), 764, 769; Kuchins and Zevelev, "Russian Foreign Policy," 155.

28. Stephen R. Weisman, "Just When It's Needed, Russia's Not There," *New York Times*, April 9, 2006.

29. "How Much Europe Depends on Russian Energy," *New York Times*, updated September 2, 2014, www.nytimes.com/interactive/2014/03/21/world/europe/how-much-europe-depends-on-russian-energy.html (retrieved August 14, 2015).

30. Goldman, *Petrostate*, 156–160.

THREE

A Chain of Unfortunate Events

1. Roxburgh, *The Strongman*, 259; Vladimir Socor, "Maidan's Ashes, Ukrainian Phoenix—A Net Assessment of the Regime Change in Ukraine Since the Start of 2014," *Eurasia Daily Monitor*, vol. 11, issue 184, October 17, 2014.

2. Andrey Kurkov, "Ukraine's Revolution: Making Sense of a Year of Chaos," BBC, November 21, 2014, www.bbc.com/news/world-europe-30131108 (retrieved November 26, 2014).

3. "Comrade Capitalism: How Russia Does Business in the Putin Era," A Reuters Investigation series, www.reuters.com/investigates/special-report/russia/#article-5-the-kiev-connection (retrieved November 26, 2014); Lally Weymouth, "Interview with Ukrainian Presidential Candidate Petro Poroshenko," *Washington Post*, April 25, 2014; Shaun Walker, "Ukraine Oligarch

Claims US Extradition Request Is Political Interference," *The Guardian*, May 5, 2015, www.theguardian.com/world/2015/may/05/ukraine-oligarch-bro kered-deal-petro-poroshenko-president-dmytro-firtash (retrieved May 6, 2015).

4. Harriet Alexander and Christopher Miller, "John McCain in Kiev: 'Ukraine will make Europe better'," *The Telegraph*, December 15, 2013, www.tele graph.co.uk/news/worldnews/europe/ukraine/10518859/John-McCain-in -Kiev-Ukraine-will-make-Europe-better.html (retrieved April 2, 2014).

5. Nina Mandell, "Vladimir Putin Calls Sen. John McCain 'Crazy,' Trashes Russian Election Protesters," *New York Daily News*, December 15, 2011, www.nydailynews.com/news/world/vladimir-putin-calls-sen-john-mccain -crazy-trashes-russian-election-protesters-article-1.992010 (retrieved March 3, 2014).

6. Victoria Nuland, "Remarks at the U.S.-Ukraine Foundation Conference," U.S. Department of State, December 13, 2013, www.state.gov/p/eur/rls/ rm/2013/dec/218804.htm (retrieved November 18, 2014); Victoria Nuland, Interview with Christiane Amanpour, April 21, 2014, IIP, April 23, 2014, http:// iipdigital.usembassy.gov/st/english/texttrans/2014/04/20140423298186 .html#ixzz3JT8maijy (retrieved November 18, 2014).

7. "Lavrov rasskazal o vrednom vliyanii Nuland na ukrainskii krizis," Lenta. ru, October 9, 2014, http://lenta.ru/news/2014/10/09/nonuland (retrieved October 9, 2014).

8. "U.S. Assistant Secretary of State Victoria Nuland Visits Independence Square," Radio Free Europe/Radio Liberty, December 11, 2013, www.rferl .org/media/video/25197233.html (retrieved November 22, 2014); Nuland, Interview with Christiane Amanpour.

9. "Ukraine Crisis: Transcript of Leaked Nuland-Pyatt Call," BBC, February 7, 2014, www.bbc.com/news/world-europe-26079957 (retrieved November 18, 2014).

10. Anthony Faiola, "Germans Not Amused by Victoria Nuland Gaffe," *Washington Post*, February 7, 2014; Ambassador Geoffrey Pyatt's Interview with CNN, February 18, 2014, Embassy of the United States, Kyiv, Ukraine, http://ukraine.usembassy.gov/speeches/cnn-02192014.html (retrieved November 18, 2014).

11. "Agreement on the Settlement of Crisis in Ukraine—full text," *The Guardian*, February 21, 2014, www.theguardian.com/world/2014/feb/21/agree ment-on-the-settlement-of-crisis-in-ukraine-full-text (retrieved September 17, 2014).

12. Andrew Higgins and Andrew E. Kramer, "Defeated Even Before He Was Ousted," *New York Times*, January 4, 2015.

13. "Rossiyane nazvali Turtsiyu liubimeishim kurortom," Lenta.ru, October 8, 2014, http://lenta.ru/news/2014/10/08/turkeystillrules (retrieved 8 October, 2014).

14. "Ukraine, Putin, and the West," *N+1*, Spring 2014, https://nplusonemag.com /issue-19/the-intellectual-situation/ukraine-putin-and-the-west/ (retrieved April 23, 2014); Stephen F. Cohen, "Distorting Russia," *The Nation*, March 3, 2014.

FOUR
History

1. Elizabeth Craven, *A Journey Through the Crimea to Constantinople* (London: Robinson, 1789), 162; Brian G. Williams, *The Crimean Tatars: The Diaspora Experience and the Forging of a Nation* (Leiden: Brill, 2001), 88.
2. *The Journey of William of Rubruck to the Eastern Parts of the World, 1253–55* (London: The Hakluyt Society, 1900), 51.
3. *The Black Sea Pilot* (Washington: Hydrographic Office, U.S. Navy, 1920), 205; Edward R. Stettinius, *Roosevelt and the Russians: The Yalta Conference* (Garden City, New York: Doubleday, 1949), 81.
4. *The Journey of William of Rubruck*, 51; Williams, *The Crimean Tatars*, 15–16; Edward N. Luttwak, *The Grand Strategy of the Byzantine Empire* (Cambridge, Mass.: The Belknap Press, 2009), 32.
5. Williams, *The Crimean Tatars*, 14–16; Maria Guthrie, *A Tour, Performed in the Years 1795–96, Through the Taurida, or Crimea* (London: Cadell and Davies, 1802), 52.
6. Pyotr Keppen, *Krymskii sbornik. O drevnostyakh yuzhnago berega Kryma i gor Tavricheskikh* (St. Petersburg: Imperatorskaya Akademiya Nauk, 1837), 45, 57; Maria A. Sosnogorova, *Putevoditel' po Krymu dlia puteshestvennikov* (Odessa: L. Nichte), 1871, 125.
7. Marco Polo, *The Travels* (Köln: Könemann, 1996), 10; *The Journey of William of Rubruck*, 51.
8. Pero Tafur, *Travels and Adventures (1435–1439)* (London: G. Routledge, 1926), 132–134; *The Journey of William of Rubruck*, 50; Keppen, *Krymskii sbornik*, 176; Steven A. Epstein, *Genoa and the Genoese, 958–1528* (Chapel Hill: University of North Carolina Press, 1996), 193, 267; A. Bezchinsky, *Putevoditel' po Krymu* (Moscow: I. N. Kushnerev, 1908), 379.
9. Tafur, *Travels and Adventures*, 132–134.
10. Epstein, *Genoa and the Genoese*, 211–212.
11. Williams, *The Crimean Tatars*, 13.
12. Ibid., 12.
13. Evliyá Efendí [Evliya Celebi], *Narratives of Travels in Europe, Asia, and Africa in the Seventeenth Century* (London: Oriental Translation Fund, 1834), 92–93. Williams, *The Crimean Tatars*, 46; Yury Shutov, *Arabatskaya strelka* (Simferopol: Tavria, 1983).

14. Lord Kinross, *Ottoman Centuries* (New York: Harper, 1979), 262–263.

15. "Opisanie Kryma (Tartariae descriptio) Martyna Bronevskogo," *Zapiski Odesskogo Obshchestva Istorii i Drevnostei*, vol. 6 (1867), 333–367; Keppen, *Krymskii sbornik*, 27–28; Williams, *The Crimean Tatars*, 56.

16. Henry A. S. Dearborn, *A Memoir on the Commerce and Navigation of the Black Sea, and Trade and Maritime Geography of Turkey and Egypt* (Boston: Wells and Lilly, 1819), vol. 2, 16; Williams, *The Crimean Tatars*, 53.

17. Nicholas V. Riasanovsky and Mark D. Steinberg, *A History of Russia* (New York: Oxford University Press, 2011), 96; John T. Alexander, *Catherine the Great: Life and Legend* (New York: Oxford University Press, 1989), 129; Kinross, *Ottoman Centuries*, 262; Simon Sebag Montefiore, *Potemkin: Catherine the Great's Imperial Partner* (New York: Vintage, 2005), 24; Alan W. Fisher, *The Crimean Tatars* (Stanford, Calif.: Hoover Institution Press, 1987), 14; Peter Hopkirk, *The Great Game: The Struggle for Empire in Central Asia* (New York: Kodansha, 1992),15.

18. Fisher, *The Crimean Tatars*, 14; Williams, *The Crimean Tatars*, 48.

19. Guthrie, *A Tour*, 213–214.

20. Williams, *The Crimean Tatars*, 26.

21. Ibid., 29, 58.

22. Isabel de Madariaga, *Ivan the Terrible: First Tsar of Russia* (New Haven: Yale University Press, 2005), 266; Williams, *The Crimean Tatars*, 49–50.

23. Williams, *The Crimean Tatars*, 51.

24. Descriptions of the Crimean Khanate can be found in a number of travelogues: Evliyá Efendí; Robert Dankoff and Sooyong Kim, eds., *An Ottoman Traveller: Selections from the Book of Travels of Evliya Celebi* (London: Eland, 2011); François Tott, *Mémoires du baron de Tott sur les Turcs et les Tartares* (Paris, 1786).

25. Joseph Brodsky, "Flight from Byzantium," in Joseph Brodsky, *Less Than One* (New York: Farrar, Straus and Giroux, 1986), 446.

26. James H. Billington, *The Icon and the Axe: An Interpretive History of Russian Culture* (New York: Vintage, 1970), 58; Madariaga, *Ivan the Terrible*, 10–11; 21.

27. Anna Komnene, *The Alexiad* (New York: Penguin, 1969), xix.

28. Madariaga, *Ivan the Terrible*, 17–19; Catherine Merridale, *Red Fortress: History and Illusion in the Kremlin* (New York: Metropolitan, 2013), 49–64; Komnene, *The Alexiad*, 39, 397.

29. Anderson, *Imagined Communities*, 15, 17.

30. Alexander, *Catherine the Great*, 247; Orlando Figes, *The Crimean War: A History* (New York: Picador, 2010), 13; Montefiore, *Potemkin*, 219–220, 242.

31. Montefiore, *Potemkin*, 246–247.

32. Ibid., 363–381; Henri Troyat, *Catherine the Great* (New York: Meridian, 1994), 272–288. Primary sources include Louis Philippe Ségur, *Mémoires*,

ou souvenirs et anecdotes (Paris, 1827) and *The Prince de Ligne: His Memoirs, Letters, and Miscellaneous Papers* (New York: Brentano's, 1899).

33. Pavel I. Sumarokov, *Dosugi krymskogo sud'yi ili Vtoroe puteshestvie v Tavridu* (St. Petersburg: Imperatorskaya Tipografiya, 1803), 130–131, 171–179; Williams, *The Crimean Tatars*, 83.

34. N. S. Vsevolozhskii, *Puteshestvie, chrez yuzhnuyu Rossiyu, Krym i Odessu, v Konstantinopol, Maluyu Aziyu, Severnuyu Afriku, Maltu, Sitsiliyu, Italiyu, yuzhnuyu Frantsiyu i Parizh v 1836 i 1837 godakh* (Moscow: Avgust Semyon, 1839), 59–79.

35. Mary Holderness, *Journey from Riga to the Crimea: With Some Accounts of the Manners and Customs of the Colonists of New Russia* (London: Sherwood, Gilbert and Piper, 1827), 216.

36. Ibid., 141, 217, 270.

37. Ibid., 145.

38. Ibid., 160–162.

39. Ibid., 163, 168, 175.

40. Ibid., 178–179.

41. Ibid., 182, 291–292.

42. Henderson, *Biblical Researches*, 289–291, 331; Mara Kozelsky, *Christianizing Crimea: Shaping Sacred Space in the Russian Empire and Beyond* (DeKalb: Northern Illinois University Press, 2010), 38.

43. Williams, *The Crimean Tatars*, 115–128; Kozelsky, *Christianizing Crimea*, 70–75.

44. Figes, *The Crimean War*, xxiii; Hopkirk, *The Great Game*, 286–287; Edward D. Clarke, *Travels in Various Countries of Europe, Asia, and Africa* (London: T. Cadell and W. Davies, 1818), 144–145.

45. Hopkirk, *The Great Game*, 286.

46. Figes, *The Crimean War*, xix, 489; Kinross, *Ottoman Centuries*, 497; William Howard Russell, *The Crimean War as Seen By Those Who Reported It* (Baton Rouge: Louisiana State University Press, 2009); Sue M. Goldie, ed., *Florence Nightingale: Letters from the Crimea, 1854–1856* (Manchester: Mandolin, 1997); Leo Tolstoy, *The Sebastopol Sketches* (New York: Penguin, 1986).

47. Williams, *The Crimean Tatars*, 146.

48. Ibid., 156, 173.

49. Anna Moskvich, *Prakticheskii putevoditel' po Krymu* (Yalta: N. P. Petrov, 1889), 6; Princess Yelena Gorchakova, *Vospominaniya o Kryme* (Moscow: Tipografiya Obshchestva Rasprostraneniya Poleznykh Knig, 1884), vol. 2, 28; Yevgeny Markov, *Ocherki Kryma. Kartiny krymskoi zhizni, istorii i prirody* (Simferopol: Tavriya, 1995), 121.

50. Markov, *Ocherki Kryma*, 122–125; Vsevolozhskii, *Puteshestvie, chrez yuzhnuyu Rossiyu*, 30–31; A. N. Nilidin, *Siluety Kryma* (St. Petersburg: Shreder, 1884), 28–29.

51. John C. Perry and Constantine Pleshakov, *The Flight of the Romanovs: A Family Saga* (New York: Basic, 1999), 46–47; P. I. Kovalevsky, *Yalta* (St. Petersburg: Arkhiv psikhiatrii, neirologii i sudebnoi psikhopatologii, 1898), 54, 133–140; Moskvich, *Prakticheskii putevoditel' po Krymu*, 160; Karl Baedeker, *Russia: A Handbook for Travelers* (Leipzig: Karl Baedeker, 1914), 405; Nilidin, *Siluety Kryma*, 17–21.

52. Harry de Windt, *Russia as I Know It* (Philadelphia: J. B. Lippincott, 1917), 184.

53. Williams, *The Crimean Tatars*, 339–342.

54. Maksimilian Voloshin, *Istoriya moei dushi* (Moscow: Agraf, 2000), 309–351; A. S. Puchenkov, "Nabokov V. D. 'Krym v 1918/19 gg.,'" *Noveishaya istoriya Rossii/Modern History of Russia*, 2015, #1, 236; M. M. Vinaver, *Nashe pravitelstvo: krymskiye vospominaniya 1918–1919 gg.* (Paris: Imprimerie d'art Voltaire, 1928); MacMillan, *Paris 1919*, 72.

55. Y. A. Slashchov-Krymskii, *Belyi Krym 1920 g. Memuary i dokumenty* (Moscow: Nauka, 1990), 131, 211–212.

56. Williams, *The Crimean Tatars*, 350.

57. Ibid., 337, 355–356; Greta Lynn Uehling, *Beyond Memory: The Crimean Tatars' Deportation and Return* (New York: Palgrave, 2004), 37.

58. Fisher, *The Crimean Tatars*, 152.

59. Gottlob Herbert Bidermann, *In Deadly Combat: A German Soldier's Memoir of the Eastern Front* (Lawrence: University Press of Kansas, 2000), 89–144; Karl Doenitz, *Memoirs: Ten Years and Twenty Days* (Annapolis, Md.: Naval Institute Press, 1990), 385–388; Manstein, *Lost Victories*, 204–259.

60. Fisher, *The Crimean Tatars*, 155–156; Williams, *The Crimean Tatars*, 376–380; V. E. Potekhin and D. V. Potekhin, *Kultura narodov Kryma* (Sevastopol, 1997), 17.

61. Fisher, *The Crimean Tatars*, 157–158.

62. Anne Applebaum, *Gulag: A History* (New York: Doubleday, 2003), 428; Williams, *The Crimean Tatars*, 405; Potekhin and Potekhin, *Kultura narodov Kryma*, 4–13.

63. Stettinius, *Roosevelt and the Russians*, 81; Charles E. Bohlen, *Witness to History, 1929–1969* (New York: Norton, 1973), 173; Mary Soames, ed., *Winston and Clementine: The Personal Letters of the Churchills* (Boston: Houghton Mifflin, 1999), 510.

64. Simon Sebag Montefiore, *Stalin: The Court of the Red Tsar* (New York: Alfred A. Knopf, 2004), 546.

65. S. M. Chervonnaya, *Tiurkskii mir yugo-vostochnoi Evropy. Krym—Severnyi Kavkaz* (Berlin: Das Arabische Buch, 2000), 77; Williams, *The Crimean Tatars*, 405.

66. Williams, *The Crimean Tatars*, 32.

67. William Taubman, *Khrushchev: The Man and His Era* (New York: W. W. Norton, 2003), 186.

FIVE
Fetish

1. *The Portable Karl Marx* (New York: Penguin, 1983), 444, 449.
2. Nikolai Nekrasov, "The Capitals Are Rocked with Thunder . . . ," in *Russian Poets*, ed. Peter Washington (New York: Alfred A. Knopf, 2009), 92.
3. V. P. Kupchenko, *Trudy i dni Maksimiliana Voloshina: Letopis' zhizni i tvorchestva, 1877–1916* (St. Petersburg: Aleteia, 2002), 25, 26; Brodsky, "Vtoroye Rozhdestvo . . . ," in Iosif Brodsky, *Sochineniya Iosifa Brodskogo* (St. Petersburg: Pushkinsky fond, 1992–2000), vol. 2, 264; Brodsky, "Zimnim vecherom v Yalte," in Brodsky, *Sochineniya*, vol. 2, 141.
4. As on January 26, 2015: Timeanddate.com, January 26, 2015, www.timeand date.com/weather (retrieved January 27, 2015).
5. Vladimir Nabokov, *Lectures on Russian Literature* (New York: Harvest, 1981), 248, 257; Vladimir Nabokov, *The Stories of Vladimir Nabokov* (New York: Vintage, 1996), 413–429.
6. P. S. Pallas, *Travels Through the Southern Provinces of the Russian Empire, in the Years 1793 and 1794* (London: John Stockdale, 1812), vol. 2, 41.
7. Kupchenko, *Trudy i dni Maksimiliana Voloshina*, 26.
8. Voloshin, *Istoriya moei dushi*, 272–273; Brodsky, "S vidom na more" ("A Place with a Sea View"), in Brodsky, *Sochineniya*, vol. 2, 158–160.
9. Kupchenko, *Trudy i dni Maksimiliana Voloshina*, 26; D. I. Shcherbakov, *Po goram Kryma, Kavkaza i Srednei Azii* (Moscow: Gosudarstvennoe izdatelstvo geograficheskoi literatury, 1954), 60.
10. Curtis, *Manuscripts Don't Burn*, 199.
11. Kupchenko, *Trudy i dni Maksimiliana Voloshina*, 5; T. Zhukovskaya and E. Kallo, eds., *"Serebryanyi vek" v Krymu: vzgliad iz XXI stoletiya. Materialy Shestykh Gertsykovskikh chtenii v g. Sudake, 8–12 iunya 2009 goda* (Moscow: Dom-musei Tsvetaevoi, 2011).
12. Adam Mickiewicz, *Sonnets from the Crimea* (San Francisco: Paul Elder, 1917).
13. "K moriu" ("Homage to the Sea"): A. S. Pushkin, *Polnoye sobraniye sochinenii v shestnadtsati tomakh* (Moscow: AN SSSR, 1937–1959), vol. 2, 331–333.
14. "Taman'": M. Yu. Lermontov, *Geroi nashego vremeni* (Moscow: Shkola-Press, 1999), 55, 63; Mikhail Lermontov, *A Hero of Our Time* (New York: Everyman's Library, 1992), 70, 81.
15. Robert Graves, *The Greek Myths* (New York: Penguin, 2012), 435–441, 594–598, 675–683.
16. "A Nereid": Pushkin, *Polnoye sobraniye sochinenii*, vol. 2, 156; Mandelshtam, "Zolotistogo myoda struia . . ." ("A string of golden honey . . ."): Osip Mandelshtam, *Polnoye sobranie stikhotvorenii* (St. Petersburg: Akademicheskii proekt, 1996), 139.
17. Brodsky, "Vtoroye Rozhdestvo . . ." ("A second Christmas"): Brodsky, *Sochi-*

neniya, vol. 2, 264; Brodsky, "Zimnim vecherom v Yalte" ("On a winter night in Yalta"): Brodsky, *Sochineniya*, vol. 2, 141.

18. Pushkin, *Polnoye sobraniye sochinenii*, vol. 4, 153–176.

19. Edward W. Said, *Orientalism* (New York: Vintage, 1979), 7; Vladimir Nabokov, *Speak, Memory* (New York: Vintage, 1989), 244.

20. A. I. Kuprin, *Izbrannye sochineniya* (Moscow: OLMA-PRESS, 2003), 660–717; Aleksandr Grin, *Alye parusa* (Moscow: Ripol Klassik, 2011); Konstantin Paustovsky, *Povest' o zhizni* (Moscow: Sinergia, 2007).

21. Shcherbakov, *Po goram Kryma*, 3–4; Brodsky, "Posvyashchaetsya Yalte" ("Homage to Yalta"): Brodsky, *Sochineniya*, vol. 2, 142–156.

22. "Khorosho!" ("All Right!"): V. V. Mayakovsky, *Sobraniye sochinenii v vosmi tomakh* (Moscow: Pravda, 1968), vol. 5, 438–439.

23. Mandelshtam, "Kholodnaya vesna . . ." ("A cold spring . . . "): Mandelshtam, 224; Mikhail Bulgakov, *Flight and Bliss* (New York: New Directions, 1985), 1–96. The movie *Beg* (1970): directed by Aleksandr Alov and Vladimir Naumov.

24. Slashchov, *Belyi Krym*, 179–180, 194–195; P. J. Capelotti, ed., *Our Man in the Crimea: Commander Hugo Koehler and the Russian Civil War* (Columbia: University of South Carolina Press, 1991), 111–112.

25. Thomas Milner, *The Crimea, Its Ancient and Modern History: The Khans, the Sultans, and the Czars* (London: Longman, Brown, Green, and Longmans, 1855), 322; Henderson, *Biblical Researches*, 361; A. Bezchinsky, *Putevoditel' po Krymu* (Moscow: I. N. Kushnerev, 1908), 214–215.

26. Xavier Hommaire de Hell, *Travels in the Steppes of the Caspian Sea, the Crimea, the Caucasus, etc* (London: Chapman and Hall, 1847), 202; Charles Henry Scott, *The Baltic, the Black Sea, and the Crimea* (London: Richard Bentley, 1854), 240.

27. Mark Twain, *The Innocents Abroad* (New York: Modern Library, 2003), 286–289; Perry and Pleshakov, *The Flight of the Romanovs*, 46–47, 176–177.

28. Katharine Blanche Guthrie, *Through Russia: From St. Petersburg to Astrakhan and the Crimea* (London: Hurst and Blackett, 1874), vol. 2, 160; Perry and Pleshakov, *The Flight of the Romanovs*, 216–218.

29. Guthrie, *Through Russia*, vol. 2, 159–160; Mrs. William Grey, *Journal of a Visit to Egypt, Constantinople, the Crimea, Greece, &c in the Suite of the Prince and Princess of Wales* (London: Smith, Elder, 1869), 186; Twain, *The Innocents Abroad*, 285.

30. Chekhov's letter to Ivan Orlov, February 22, 1899: Lillian Hellman, ed., *The Selected Letters of Anton Chekhov* (New York: Barnes & Noble, 2007), 236.

31. "The Lady with the Dog": Anton Chekhov, *Stories* (New York: Bantam, 2000), 361–376.

32. "Big Mouth" ("*Dlinnyi yazyk*"): A. P. Chekhov, *Polnoye sobraniye sochinenii* (Moscow: AN SSSR, 1979–1982), vol. 5, 313–316; Vladimir V. Svyatlovsky, *Yuzhnyi bereg Kryma i Riviera* (St. Petersburg: A. S. Suvorin, 1902), 119–121.

33. "Putin i Timoshenko uzhnali u Rotaru i smeyalis' nad Yushchenko i galstukami Mikho," *Segodnya.ua*, November 20, 2009, www.segodnya.ua/ukraine/putin -i-timoshenko-uzhnali-u-rotaru-i-cmejalic-nad-jushchenko-i-halctukami -mikho.html (retrieved May 2, 2015).

34. Figes, *The Crimean War*, xvii.

35. L. N. Tolstoy, Dnevniki i zapisnye knizhki, 1854–1857: *Polnoye sobraniye sochinenii* (Moscow: Khudozhestvennaya literatura, 1937), vol. 47, 37, 48, 56–57; Tolstoy, *The Sebastopol Sketches.*

36. Twain, *The Innocents Abroad*, 279; Grey, *Journal of a Visit to Egypt*, 173.

37. Akhmatova, "U samogo morya . . ." ("On the sea coast . . . "): Anna Akhmatova, *Stikhotvoreniya i poemy* (Leningrad: Sovetskii pisatel, 1977), 339–340.

38. G. K. Zhukov, *Vospominaniya i razmyshleniya* (Moscow: Olma-Press, 2002), vol. 1, 263–264; A. M. Vasilevsky, *Delo vsei zhizni* (Moscow: Olma-Press, 2002), 371; Bidermann, *In Deadly Combat*, 142.

39. Vasilevsky, *Delo vsei zhizni*, 371; N. G. Kuznetsov, *Kursom k pobede* (Moscow: Olma-Press, 2003), 189.

40. Luttwak, *The Grand Strategy*, 121–122; Milner, *The Crimea*, 116.

41. Kozelsky, *Christianizing Crimea*, 78–117.

42. Constantine Pleshakov, *The Tsar's Last Armada: The Epic Journey to the Battle of Tsushima* (New York: Basic, 2000).

SIX
The Takeover

1. "Chto takoe Krym: tsifry i fakty," Allcrimea.net, March 8, 2014, http:// news.allcrimea.net/news/2014/3/8/chto-takoe-krym-tsifry-i-fakty-6949 (retrieved November 11, 2014).

2. Matlock, *Autopsy of an Empire*, 701–702.

3. Anna Reid, *Borderland: A Journey Through the History of Ukraine* (Boulder, Colo.: Westview, 2000), 171–173.

4. Chervonnaya, *Tiurkskii mir yugo-vostochnoi Evropy*, 77.

5. Roland Oliphant, "Ukraine's Defence Chief Resigns as Troops Leave Crimea," *The Telegraph*, March 25, 2014, www.telegraph.co.uk/news/worldnews/europe /ukraine/10722676/Ukraines-defence-chief-resigns-as-troops-leave-Crimea .html (retrieved April 18, 2015).

6. Montefiore, *Potemkin*, 244; Williams, *The Crimean Tatars*, 9, 33–35.

7. Ibid., 49–50.

8. Ibid., 51.

9. Ibid., 53.

10. Uehling, *Beyond Memory*, 44.

11. Chervonnaya, *Tiurkskii mir yugo-vostochnoi Evropy*, 61–62.

12. Ibid., 58.

13. John C. K. Daly, "After Crimea: The Future of the Black Sea Fleet," *The Jamestown Foundation*, May 22, 2014; Vladimir Putin's interview in a documentary, "Crimea: A Way Home," Gazeta.ru, March 15, 2015, www.gazeta.ru/politics/2015/03/15_a_6600065.shtml (retrieved April 17, 2015).

14. "About the Republic," Official Tatarstan (Tatarstan.ru), http://tatarstan.ru/eng/about/population.htm (retrieved April 18, 2015).

15. Robert D. Crews, "Moscow and the Mosque: Co-opting Muslims in Putin's Russia," *Foreign Affairs*, March/April 2014.

16. Marc Weller, "Why Russia's Crimea Move Fails Legal Test," BBC, March 7, 2014, www.bbc.com/news/world-europe-26481423 (retrieved February 16, 2015).

17. David Axe and Robert Beckhusen, "NATO Could Have Trouble Combating Putin's Military Strategy," Reuters, September 15, 2014, http://blogs.reuters.com/great-debate/2014/09/15/how-nato-could-defend-against-a-russian-invasion (retrieved December 4, 2014).

18. The February 2013 article in *Voyenno-promyshlennyi vestnik* by the chief of the Russian General Staff, Valery Gerasimov: Mark Galeotti, "The 'Gerasimov Doctrine' and Russian Non-Linear War," In Moscow's Shadows: Analysis and Assessment of Russian Crime and Security, July 6, 2014, http://inmoscowsshadows.wordpress.com/2014/07/06/the-gerasimov-doctrine-and-russian-non-linear-war (retrieved December 4, 2014).

19. Ron Synovitz, "Russian Forces in Crimea: Who Are They and Where Did They Come From?" Radio Free Europe/Radio Liberty, March 4, 2014, www.rferl.org/content/russian-forces-in-crimea--who-are-they-and-where-did-they-come-from/25285238.html (retrieved April 18, 2015); Putin's interview in the documentary "Crimea: A Way Home," Gazeta.ru, March 15, 2015, www.gazeta.ru/politics/2015/03/15_a_6600065.shtml (retrieved April 17, 2015); Jeremy Hsu, "'Ambiguous' Warfare Buys Upgrade Time for Russia's Military," *Scientific American*, August 12, 2014; "Ukraine to Lose Offshore Gas Fields in Black Sea," B92.net, Internet news site of Serbian radio outlet, www.b92.net/eng/news/world.php?yyyy=2014&mm=03&dd=20&nav_id=89717, March 20, 2014 (retrieved March 23, 2014).

20. Philip Shishkin, "One-Ship Ukraine Navy Defies Russia to the End," *Wall Street Journal*, updated March 26, 2014, www.wsj.com/articles/SB10001424052702303949704579461513462696086 (retrieved May 10, 2016).

21. "Russia Parades Bastion-P in Crimea," Asian Defense News, May 18, 2014, http://asian-defence-news.blogspot.com/2014/05/russia-parades-bastion-p-in-crimea.html (retrieved May 10, 2016).

22. "Ukraine's Military Bases Targeted in Crimea," Radio Free Europe/Radio Liberty, March 22, 2014, www.rferl.org/content/ukraine-crimea-bases-targetted/25306141.html (retrieved April 18, 2015).

23. Charles Recknagel, "Explainer: How Do Russia's and Ukraine's Armies Compare?" Radio Free Europe/Radio Liberty, March 6, 2014, www.rferl.org/content/russia-ukraine-armies-compare/25287910.html (retrieved April 18, 2015).

24. "Mikhail Gorbachev Hails Crimea Annexation," United Press International, March 18, 2014, www.upi.com/Top_News/World-News/2014/03/18/Mikhail-Gorbachev-hails-Crimea-annexation-to-Russia/6881395193402 (retrieved May 10, 2016); "Grand Duchess Maria: Russia Will Not Give Up Crimea Despite Sanctions," Russia Beyond the Headlines, April 17, 2014, http://rbth.com/international/2014/04/17/grand_duchess_maria_russia_will_not_give_up_crimea_despite_sanc_35993.html?code=53cc7f85fa6d4bf192901d08a80d4a5a (retrieved July 1, 2014).

SEVEN

From Crimea to Donbass

1. Nicholas Kristof, "Moldova, the Next Ukraine," *New York Times*, April 23, 2014.

2. Nick Cumming-Bruce, "Death Toll in Ukraine Conflict Hits 9,160, U.N. Says," *New York Times*, March 3, 2016.

3. Andrew S. Weiss, "Putin the Improviser," *Wall Street Journal*, February 20, 2015.

4. Michael R. Gordon, "Russia Displays a New Military Prowess in Ukraine's East," *New York Times*, April 21, 2014.

5. "Strelkov priznal otvetstvennost' za voyennye deistviya na Ukraine," Lenta.ru, November 20, 2014, http://lenta.ru/news/2014/11/20/strelkov (retrieved November 20, 2014).

6. David Stern, "Ukraine Underplays Role of Far Right in Conflict," BBC, December 13, 2014, www.bbc.com/news/world-europe-30414955 (retrieved December 13, 2014).

7. Tim Whewell, "The Russians Fighting a 'Holy War' in Ukraine," BBC, December 17, 2014, www.bbc.com/news/magazine-30518054 (retrieved December 18, 2014); Joshua Yaffa, "The Inconvenient Soldier," *New York Times Magazine*, January 11, 2015, p. 49.

8. Andrew Roth, "Ukrainians in the Battered East Scramble in Darkness as Winter Nears," *New York Times*, November 1, 2014.

9. "Eto ne plata za Krym, eto plata za samosokhraneniye," Gazeta.ua, December 18, 2014, http://gazeta.ua/ru/articles/politics/_eto-ne-plata-za-krym-eto-plata-za-samosohranenie-putin-o-krizise-v-rf/599495 (retrieved December 19, 2014).

10. "Vladimir Putin Press Conference," *The Guardian*, December 17, 2015.

11. "Ukraine Crisis," BBC, November 22, 2014, www.bbc.com/news/world-eu rope-30158978 (retrieved November 22, 2014).

12. "Voennaya doktrina Rossiiskoi Federatsii," *Rossiiskaya gazeta*, December 30, 2014, www.rg.ru/2014/12/30/doktrina-dok.html (retrieved January 9, 2015).

13. *Kapitanskaya dochka (The Captain's Daughter)*: Pushkin, *Polnoye sobraniye sochinenii*, vol. 8, 277–384.

14. "Fragile States Index: The Indicators," Fund for Peace, http://fsi.fundfor peace.org/indicators (retrieved May 11, 2016).

15. "Ukraine: UN Warns Number of Displaced Persons and Refugees on the Rise," U.N. News Centre, June 18, 2015, www.un.org/apps/news/story.asp? NewsID=51193#.VdXfjyxViko (retrieved August 20, 2015).

16. Stern, "Ukraine Underplays Role of Far Right"; "Death Toll Rises to Three from Grenade Attack Near Ukrainian Parliament," Radio Free Europe/ Radio Liberty, September 1, 2015, www.rferl.org/content/ukraine-second -national-guardsman-dies/27220213.html (retrieved September 13, 2015).

17. David Stern, "Ukraine Clashes Raise Questions over Right Sector Militia," BBC, July 15, 2015, www.bbc.com/news/world-europe-33523869 (retrieved August 20, 2015).

18. "Pro-Kiev Militias Are Fighting Putin, but Has Ukraine Created a Monster It Can't Control?" *Vox*, updated February 20, 2015, www.vox.com/ 2015/2/20/8072643/ukraine-volunteer-battalion-danger (retrieved May 31, 2015); Alan Cullison, "Ukraine's Secret Weapon: Feisty Oligarch Ihor Kolomoisky," *Wall Street Journal*, June 27, 2014.

19. Glenn Kates, "Ten Takeaways from Ukraine's Vote," Radio Free Europe/ Radio Liberty, October 27, 2014, www.rferl.org/content/ukraine-vote-take aways-things-we-learned/26659694.html (retrieved October 29, 2014); Leonid Bershidsky, "Ukraine's Truly Foreign Ministers," Bloomberg, December 3, 2014, www.bloombergview.com/articles/2014-12-03/ukraines-truly-foreign -ministers (retrieved May 31, 2015); "Ukraine Names Ex-Georgian President Saakashvili as Odessa Governor," *The Guardian*, May 31, 2015.

20. "Poslaniye presidenta Federalnomu Sobraniyu. 4 dekabrya 2014 g.," Krem lin.ru, December 4, 2014, http://kremlin.ru/news/47173 (retrieved January 9, 2015).

21. "Nato Commander Warns Russia Could Control Whole Black Sea," BBC, November 26, 2014, www.bbc.com/news/world-europe-30214172 (retrieved November 26, 2014).

22. Doenitz, *Memoirs*, 389.

23. Orhan Pamuk, *Istanbul: Memories and the City* (New York: Vintage, 2006), 203.

24. "United Nations Convention on the Law of the Sea of 10 December 1982," United Nations, updated August 22, 2013, www.un.org/depts/los/convention _agreements/convention_overview_convention.htm (retrieved February 8,

2015); William J. Broad, "In Taking Crimea, Putin Gains a Sea of Fuel Reserves," *New York Times*, May 17, 2014.

25. Darya Korsunskaya, "Putin Drops South Stream Gas Pipeline to EU, Courts Turkey," Reuters, December 1, 2014, www.reuters.com/article/2014/12/01/us-russia-gas-gazprom-pipeline-idUSKCN0JF30A20141201 (retrieved December 1, 2014).

26. Elena Mazneva and James Kraus, "Gazprom to Buy Out Partners in Canceled South Stream Project," Bloomberg, December 29, 2014, www.bloom berg.com/news/articles/2014-12-29/gazprom-to-buy-out-eu-partners-in-canceled-south-stream-project (retrieved March 30, 2015); Elena Mazneva and Marco Bertacche, "Gazprom Said to Pay Saipem for Vessels at Dropped Black Sea Link," Bloomberg, March 6, 2015, www.bloomberg.com/news/articles/2015-03-06/gazprom-said-to-pay-saipem-for-vessels-at-dropped-black-sea-link (retrieved March 30, 2015).

27. "Chevron reshila vyiti iz slantsevogo proekta na Ukraine," Lenta.ru, December 15, 2014, http://lenta.ru/news/2014/12/15/chevron/ (retrieved December 15, 2014).

28. Fiona Harvey, "Russia 'Secretly Working with Environmentalists to Oppose Fracking'," *The Guardian*, June 19, 2014.

EIGHT
#CrimeaIsOurs

1. David M. Herszenhorn, "Kiev Blamed for Blackout in Capital of Crimea," *New York Times*, March 24, 2014; "Rossiiskiye zhurnalisty vyiasnili za schet chego zhivet ekonomika Kryma," *Novosti Kryma*, March 4, 2014, http://news.allcrimea.net/news/2014/3/4/rossiiskie-zhurnalisty-vyyasnili-za-schet-che go-zhivet-ekonomika-kryma-6529 (retrieved April 2, 2014).

2. "Pereprava v Kerchi ne budet rabotat' neskolko dnei iz-za shtorma," *Novosti Kryma*, November 19, 2014, http://news.allcrimea.net/news/2014/11/19/pereprava-v-kerchi-ne-budet-rabotat-neskolko-dnei-izza-shtorma-25747 (retrieved November 19, 2014).

3. "Kurorty Kryma otrabotali v teni," *Novosti Kryma*, October 4, 2014, http://news.allcrimea.net/news/2014/10/4/kurorty-kryma-otrabotali-v-teni-22959 (retrieved October 5, 2014); "Chto takoye Krym: tsifry i fakty," *Novosti Kryma*, March 8, 2014, http://news.allcrimea.net/news/2014/3/8/chto-takoe-krym-tsifry-i-fakty-6949/ (retrieved October 5, 2014).

4. "Kurorty Kryma otrabotali v teni"; "Krymskie kanikuly: turisticheskii sezon-2015," Forbes.ru, August 14, 2015, www.forbes.ru/sobytiya-photogallery/obshchestvo/296297-krymskie-kanikuly-turisticheskii-sezon-2015(retrieved August 21, 2015).

5. Moskvich, *Prakticheskii putevoditel' po Krymu*, 6; Tolstoy, Dnevniki i zapisnye knizhki, 48.

6. Neil MacFarquhar, "Crimean Vineyards of Last Czar Withstand Time and Tumult," *New York Times*, May 28, 2014; "Vina krymskoi 'Massandry' v Rossii nazvali vinnym napitkom," *Ekonomicheskaya Pravda*, May 28, 2014, www.epravda.com.ua/rus/news/2014/05/28/458777 (retrieved July 5, 2014); "V Krymu prekratil rabotu vinnyi zavod 'Solnechnaya Dolina'," *Novosti Kryma*, February 15, 2015, http://news.allcrimea.net/news/2015/2/15/v-krymu-prekratil-rabotu-vinnyi-zavod-solnechnaya-dolina-31344 (retrieved February 15, 2015).

7. Neil MacFarquhar, "Aid Elusive, Crimea Farms Face Hurdles," *New York Times*, July 8, 2014.

8. Neil MacFarquhar, "Seizing Assets in Crimea, from Shipyard to Film Studio," *New York Times*, January 10, 2015.

9. "Priplyli: Yalta prelstila ne vsekh nemetskikh turistov," Town of Yalta site, September 23, 2014, www.0654.com.ua/article/625700 (retrieved September 29, 2014).

10. Laurence Norman and Frances Robinson, "EU Toughens Sanctions on Crimea-Based Companies," *Wall Street Journal*, December 18, 2014; "Obama to Block Exports of Goods, Technology, Services to Crimea," Reuters, December 19, 2014, www.reuters.com/article/2014/12/19/us-ukraine-crisis-obama-idUSKBN0JX2DG20141219 (retrieved December 20, 2014).

11. "Izbirkomy Kryma i Sevastopolya utverdili ofitsialnye rezultaty vyborov," Russkaya sluzhba novostei, September 16, 2014, www.rusnovosti.ru/news/341297 (retrieved September 16, 2014); "Yavka na vyborakh v Mosgordumu sostavila okolo 20%," *Argumenty i fakty*, September 15, 2014, www.aif.ru/politics/russia/1337910 (retrieved September 16, 2014); "Mosgorizbirkom utverdil rezultaty vyborov v Moskovskuyu gorodskuyu dumu VI sozyva," ITAR-TASS, September 16, 2014, http://itar-tass.com/politika/1445988 (retrieved September 16, 2014).

12. "Dzhemilev zayavlyaet, chto Medzhlis mozhet uiti v podpolye v Krymu," Finance.ua, May 9, 2014, http://news.finance.ua/ru/news/-/325148/dzhemilev-zayavlyaet-chto-medzhlis-mozhet-ujti-v-podpole-v-krymu (retrieved August 21, 2015).

13. "Concerns Raised over Crimean Tatars Fighting with IS," Radio Free Europe/Radio Liberty, November 19, 2014, www.rferl.org/content/concerns-raised-over-crimean-tatars-fighting-with-is/26699848.html (retrieved November 19, 2014); "Na storone islamskogo gosudarstva voyuyut okolo 500 krymchan," *Novosti Kryma*, November 18, 2014, http://news.allcrimea.net/news/2014/11/18/na-storone-islamskogo-gosudarstva-vojujut-okolo-500-krymchan-25692 (retrieved November 18, 2014).

14. Williams, *The Crimean Tatars*, 2.

15. David J. Kramer, President, Freedom House, Hearing of the Senate Foreign Relations Committee, *Freedom House*, May 6, 2014, https://freedomhouse.org/article/ukraine-countering-russian-intervention-and-supporting-democratic-state#.Vdc3_CxViko (retrieved August 21, 2015).
16. Craven, *A Journey Through the Crimea*, 162; Vasily Aksyonov, *Ostrov Krym* (Ann Arbor: Ardis, 1981), 270–272.
17. Potekhin and Potekhin, *Kultura narodov Kryma*, 6–30, 42.

NINE
You Break It, You Run

1. David Brooks, "Snap Out of It," *New York Times*, September 23, 2014; Ann Schneible, "War Ruins God's Creative Work, Pope Says," Catholic News Agency, September 13, 2014, www.catholicnewsagency.com/news/war-ruins-gods-creative-work-pope-says-76113 (retrieved September 14, 2014).
2. Yuval Shany, "Does International Law Grant the People of Crimea and Donetsk a Right to Secede? Revisiting Self-Determination in Light of the 2014 Events in Ukraine," *The Brown Journal of World Affairs*, Fall/Winter 2014, vol. 21, issue 1, 233.
3. Steven Pifer, "Ukraine Crisis' Impact on Nuclear Weapons," CNN, March 4, 2014, www.cnn.com/2014/03/04/opinion/pifer-ukraine-budapest-memorandum (retrieved March 8, 2015).
4. The North Atlantic Treaty (April 4, 1949, Washington, D.C.), NATO, www.nato.int/cps/en/natolive/official_texts_17120.htm (retrieved February 13, 2015).
5. Adrian Croft, "Giuliani Says NATO Should Admit Israel, Japan," Reuters, September 19, 2007, www.reuters.com/article/2007/09/19/us-iran-giuliani-idUSL1992785020070919 (retrieved February 13, 2015).
6. "Wales Summit Declaration: Issued by the Heads of State and Government Participating in the Meeting of the North Atlantic Council in Wales," NATO, September 5, 2014, www.nato.int/cps/en/natohq/official_texts_112964.htm?mode=pressrelease (retrieved December 19, 2014).
7. Ibid.; "US and NATO Troops Begin Ukraine Military Exercise," BBC, September 15, 2014, www.bbc.com/news/world-europe-29204505 (retrieved September 15, 2014); Russian Foreign Ministry press secretary Aleksandr Lukashevich's statement, Novobsor.ru, September 11, 2014, http://novoboz.ru/2014/09/11/152500 (retrieved August 21, 2015).
8. "Raketnyi esminets USS Cole i shtabnoi korabl 6-go flota SshA USS Mount Whitney vkhodyat v Chernoye more," *Black Sea News*, October 10, 2014, www.blackseanews.net/read/88801 (retrieved 11 October 2014).
9. Thomas Barrabi, "Ukraine's NATO Entrance Amid Russian Aggression 'At

Least 6–7 Years' Away, Poroshenko Says," *International Business Times,* June 30, 2015, www.ibtimes.com/ukraines-nato-entrance-amid-russian-aggression -least-6-7-years-away-poroshenko-says-1989763, June 30, 2015 (retrieved August 22, 2015).

10. "Nato Invitation to Montenegro Prompts Russia Warning," BBC, December 2, 2015, www.bbc.com/news/world-europe-34981973 (retrieved December 2, 2015).

11. Paul Craig Roberts, "Sleepwalking Again," Paul Craig Roberts Institute for Political Economy, February 22, 2014, www.paulcraigroberts.org/ 2014/02/22/sleepwalking (retrieved July 4, 2014); Damien Sharkov, "Oliver Stone Meets Toppled Ukrainian President Yanukovych, Accuses CIA of Sparking Coup," *Newsweek,* December 31, 2014, www.newsweek.com /oliver-stone-meets-toppled-ukrainian-president-accuses-cia-sparking -coup-295814 (retrieved January 6, 2015).

12. Andrew Wilson, *Ukraine Crisis: What It Means for the West* (New Haven: Yale University Press, 2014), ix; Michael A. McFaul, "Confronting Putin's Russia," *New York Times,* March 24, 2014.

13. Kagan, "Superpowers Don't Get to Retire."

14. Kissinger, "To Settle the Ukraine Crisis . . . "; Jack F. Matlock, "Who Is the Bully?" *Washington Post,* March 14, 2014.

15. Dimitri Simes and Paul Saunders, "Obama's Crimea Blunder," *Washington Times,* March 31, 2014.

16. George P. Shultz and Sam Nunn, "The U.S. Strategy for Keeping Ukraine Safe from Russian Aggression," *Washington Post,* March 27, 2014.

17. "Rossiiski proizvoditel otkrestilsya ot avarii rakety Antares," Lenta.ru, October 29, 2014, lenta.ru/news/2014/10/29/raketa (retrieved October 29, 2014).

18. Ryan Browne, "U.S. Stationing Tanks and Artillery in Classified Norwegian Caves," CNN, February 19, 2016, www.cnn.com/2016/02/18/poli tics/u-s-tanks-artillery-norwegian-caves (retrieved February 20, 2016).

19. Hugh Schofield, "Hollande in Moscow: A New Era in Russian-French Relations?" BBC, November 26, 2015, www.bbc.com/news/world-europe -34931378 (retrieved February 20, 2016).

20. "Saipem Awarded Contract for South Stream Offshore Pipeline," The Maritime Executive, March 17, 2014, www.maritime-executive.com/arti cle/Saipem-Awarded-Contract-for-South-Stream-Offshore-Pipeline -2014-03-17 (retrieved May 5, 2014).

21. "South Stream Pipeline Project Frozen over Crimea Crisis," EurActiv.com, March 11, 2014, www.euractiv.com/energy/south-stream-project-takes-crime -news-534038 (retrieved March 11, 2014); "EU Policy to Blame for Ukraine Crisis—Ex-Chancellor Schroeder," *Russia Today,* May 12, 2014, http://rt .com/news/158432-schroeder-russia-sanctions-eu (retrieved October 2, 2014); "Obama, Merkel Aim to Display Unity Against Russia," Fox News, May 2,

2014, www.foxnews.com/politics/2014/05/02/obama-merkel-to-display-unity -against-russia (retrieved May 2, 2014).

22. Nick Cunningham, "As Russia's Isolation Grows, Oil Companies Caught in Middle," July 21, 2014, EconoMonitor, www.economonitor.com/blog/ 2014/07/as-russias-isolation-grows-oil-companies-caught-in-middle/?utm_ source=rss (retrieved September 2, 2014); "Austria Says EU Must Not Seek Collapse of Russian Economy," Reuters, December 20, 2014, www.reu ters.com/article/2014/12/20/us-ukraine-crisis-russia-austria-idUSKBN 0JY0IY20141220 (retrieved December 20, 2014).

23. Judy Dempsey, "Europe's Energy Companies Go Back to Business with Rus-sia," Carnegie Europe, September 7, 2015, http://carnegieeurope.eu/strategic europe/?fa=61207 (retrieved September 13, 2015).

24. Thomas Erdbrink, "Despite Anger Over Downed Jetliner, Europe Shies Away from Sanctions on Russia," *New York Times*, July 23, 2014; Maia de la Baume, "A French Port Welcomes an Intervention by Russia's Military," *New York Times*, July 22, 2014

25. "McCain Sparks US-Hungary Diplomatic Row over Orban," BBC, December 3, 2014, www.bbc.com/news/world-europe-30318898 (retrieved December 8, 2014); Tom Porter, "Hungarian PM Viktor Orban Hits Back at John Mc-Cain's 'Fascist' Accusation," *International Business Times*, December 6, 2014, www.ibtimes.co.uk/hungarian-pm-viktor-orban-hits-back-john-mccains -fascist-accusation-1478364 (retrieved December 8, 2014).

26. Bernard-Henri Lévy, "Putin's Crime, Europe's Cowardice," *New York Times*, July 23, 2014.

27. Robert Myles, "U.S. Call for NATO to Buy French-Built Warships Des-tined for Russia," *Digital Journal*, June 2, 2014, www.digitaljournal.com/news/ world/us-call-for-nato-to-buy-french-built-warships-destined-for-russia/arti cle/385327 (retrieved November 7, 2014); Matt Millham, "Lawmakers Again Urge NATO to Buy French Warships Slated for Russia," *Stars and Stripes*, No-vember 7, 2014, www.stripes.com/news/lawmakers-again-urge-nato-to-buy -french-warships-slated-for-russia-1.312864 (retrieved November 7, 2014).

28. Susannah Cullinane and Noisette Martel, "France to Sell Egypt Two War-ships Previously Contracted to Russia," CNN, September 24, 2015, www .cnn.com/2015/09/23/europe/france-egypt-warship-sale (retrieved Septem-ber 24, 2015); "Egypt Agrees to Buy Warships Built for Russia from France," BBC, September 23, 2015, www.bbc.com/news/world-europe-34335224 (retrieved September 24, 2015).

29. Rajan Menon and Eugene Rumer, *Conflict in Ukraine: The Unwinding of the Post–Cold War Order* (Boston: MIT Press, 2015), xix.

30. Scott McConnell, "NATO's Wrong Turn," *The American Conservative*, March 28, 2014, www.theamericanconservative.com/articles/natos-wrong-turn (re-trieved November 22, 2014).

31. Jeffrey Sachs, "Viewpoint: Why the Shadow of WW1 and 1989 Hangs over World Events," December 16, 2014, *BBC Magazine*, www.bbc.com/news/magazine-30483873 (retrieved December 17, 2014).

32. Huntington, *The Clash of Civilizations*, 20–21.

33. Kissinger, "To Settle the Ukraine Crisis . . . "

34. Antoine de Saint-Exupéry, *The Little Prince*, translated by Richard Howard (New York: Harcourt, 2000), 30–31.

35. David Rothkopf, "Obama's 'Don't Do Stupid Shit' Foreign Policy," *Foreign Policy*, June 4, 2014; Jeffrey Goldberg, "Hilary Clinton: 'Failure' to Help Syrian Rebels Led to the Rise of ISIS," *The Atlantic*, August 10, 2014; Jeffrey Goldberg, "The Obama Doctrine," *The Atlantic*, April 2016; John McCain, "Salute to a Communist," *New York Times*, March 24, 2016.

36. David Remnick, "World-Weary," *New Yorker*, September 15, 2014.

Index

Index

Index